Opening and Healing the Light Body with

the Spiritual Meridian Therapy

Translated by Christine M. Grimm

LOTUS PRESS · SHANGRI-LA

Disclaimer

The methods described in this book are not meant to replace professional advice and medical treatment. Light-Channel Healing helps the body to heal itself—so it does not claim to heal diseases.

The information presented in this book has been carefully researched and passed on to the best of our knowledge and conscience. Despite this fact, neither the author nor the publisher assume any type of liability for presumed or actual damages of any child that might result from the direct or indirect application of use of the statements in this book. The information in this book is intended for interested readers and educational purposes.

First English Edition 2005
©by Lotus Press
Box 325, Twin Lakes, WI 53181, USA
website: www.lotuspress.com
email: lotuspress@lotuspress.com
The Shangri-La Series is published in cooperation
with Schneelöwe Verlagsberatung, Federal Republic of Germany
© 2001 by Windpferd Verlagsgesellschaft mbH, Aitrang, Germany
All rights reserved
Translated by Christine M. Grimm
Cover layout by Kuhn Graphik, Digitales Design, Zurich, Switzerland
Cover illustration by Michaela Nagel
Interior illustrations by Alexandra Fink-Thali and Trudi Thali
Pictures: on pages 134-147 by Peter Ehrhardt
ISBN 0-914955-78-0
Library of Congress Control Number: 2005923267

Printed in USA

TABLE OF CONTENTS

Preface

Now more than ever, humanity is confronted with problems of threatening proportions that we have never faced before. The dangers of technology, the climatic changes, and an increasingly damaged natural environment and basis of life can no longer be overlooked. Human beings are entering the previously unknown expanses of the universe, as well as the smallest building blocks of life. There is a major push for research and the motivation is often based only on short-term profits and personal success. But do the findings of our scientists really promote the well-being of humans, nature, and all living beings? Is it possible that we are risking our health and the natural basis of life through electro-smog, emissions, stress, and a hectic pace? We should never forget that everything that has manifested on the Earth is filled with an indescribable intelligence in the form of an invisible light and any violation of it will result in retribution. Changes in a negative direction, as we are now observing, occur when the natural laws of the creative intelligence are not respected.

In these times of transformation and upheaval, it is comforting to be allowed to observe how the sensitivity of human beings is developing at an enormous rate. The veils to the invisible light world are being slowly drawn aside so that things that were still concealed up until a few years ago are now perceived more frequently.

Increasingly more human beings feel connected with the energy and light of the angels. Through the force of their own consciousness, many people are starting to shape their lives anew and feel that they are interwoven with the momentary life circumstances. A new consciousness is developing in particular for our own bodies—which creates an enormous potential for the health and well-being of the body and the soul!

It was the lifting of the veil that brought me into connection with the invisible light world that equally floods every living being with light and power. As a result, it became possible for me to develop a new therapy—Light-Channel Healing. It focuses on a good flow of light and vital energy by dissolving the blockages in the meridians, which are the energy channels. It is based on the ancient Chinese meridian teachings. Meridians are energy channels in which the life force ch'i circulates in the body. They are simultaneously oriented toward a cosmic structure of order for the higher planes of light. Among other things, meridians are the foundation of acupuncture, which is being increasingly recognized and practiced even by the orthodox medical doctors today in the West. I feel that ch'i or vital energy is light. It opens us for the high vibrations of the universal Christ Light. In my many years of work and experience as a holistic health practitioner, I have discovered time and again that a gentle touch with the hands is enough to stimulate the flow in these energy channels. During the treatment, my Third Eye sees how the dissolution of blockages in the energy system produces a wonderful glowing of the colorful rainbow light. This experience gives me the certainty that Divine Light flows through the channels of our bodies in order to keep the body and soul healthy.

This new therapy is a gentle revolution in health care because it is simple, effective, and healing. It connects the light of the soul with the body. A good flow of light and strength is the foundation for holistic health.

Light-Channel work is accessible to anyone. We can use it for ourselves, as well as for others. The only thing we need is a bit of basic knowledge, loving attention, and some time. The hands serve as a wonderful, natural tool for this work.

My intention in writing this book is to show how we can improve our physical and emotional well-being through the stimulation of the energy system and by dissolving blockages. Light and strength flowing through us is not only the basis for physical health, but also brightens the soul with love, joy, and the life force. I wish my readers many positive experiences with this beneficial therapy.

Trudi Thali
Vitznau, Switzerland
Spring of 2005

Introduction

Increasing sensitivity and the expansion of consciousness inspire a growing number of people to seek true healing in the realm of subtle energy. More and more individuals have experienced impressive healing success for a great variety of health disorders through new, advanced therapies. The reason for the success of these new therapies is that they consider the soul and body to be a unified system and treat them in keeping with this perspective. I have developed Light-Channel Healing as a new therapy from the knowledge that the body is surrounded by an aura—an energy field of various light frequencies. This light is transmitted into the body through the chakras in the form of a spiral. From the energy centers, the light flows through the meridians or light channels into every cell of the body.

I was born clairsentient and can clearly feel the flow of the life force, as well as all the obstacles or blockages that prevent a harmonious flow within a human being. In the ancient Chinese methods of healing, I found a wonderful confirmation of my perceptions. So Light-Channel work creates a synthesis between the Eastern understanding of the creative basic forces of life, yin and yang, and the newly awakening light-consciousness in the West. The foundations are the magnificent perceptions of the ancient Chinese culture, the roots of which go back to more than 6000 B.C. At that time, it appears that the first emperors were priests or shamans and at the same time God-men. The connection between the cosmos and the earth runs through the entire ancient Chinese culture like a red thread: These people recognized the deep mysteries of the creative forces of the heavens and their correlations on earth.

The great sage Lao Tsu, the founder of Taoism, lived in the 6th Century B.C. The perception of two complementary basic forces, yin and yang, also characterize this view of the world in relation to the human body. The philosophy of the Tao is concerned with the ability of integrating vibrational frequencies from the higher planes into consciousness. The all-encompassing force—the Tao—was depicted as light. Bringing the polarities into harmony was their goal for a balanced life.

Even today, the great knowledge of the ancient Chinese about the laws of the creative forces in effect in both the macrocosm and the microcosm is impressive. They recognized that the cosmos and the earth, nature and the human being, created according to the same "blueprint," are a wonderful reflection of an unfathomable creative source of power. Only now are we rediscovering the deep truth of this ancient natural philosophy and are drawing on it anew.

Lung Meridian, according to an ancient Chinese drawing

Sensitivity must have been highly developed in these ancient times—how else could they have recognized the system of the yin and yang energy currents in the body! These are only visible to the spiritual eye or can be felt intuitively. The insight of that time formed an outstanding foundation for medical treatment. During the *Han Dynasty* (202 B.C.

to A.D. 220) there were maps with the exact course of the meridians. The first therapies consisted of stimulating the energy flow in the meridians with bamboo splinters and later with needles or herbs and bringing them back into harmony. The oldest work of Chinese Medicine theory, the *Yellow Emperor's Classics of Internal Medicine* was written in the 2nd Century B.C. In the meantime, recent burial finds indicate that therapeutic instruments such as stone needles or bamboo splinters were already in use 4000 or even 6000 years ago. Many medical books were written in the *Ming Dynasty* (A.D. 1368 to 1644). Today in the Western world, the foundations of the ancient Chinese way of healing are finding increased recognition as Traditional Chinese Medicine (TCM).

On the other hand, the treatment in my new energy therapy is absolutely pain-free and very relaxing. A gentle touch of the hands is enough to stimulate the light channels without needles, moxibustion, or painful stretching and pressing. The important element here is opening the consciousness for higher vibrational frequencies. Love is the strongest power in the universe, and the radiant power of the hands is increased by the light of the angels, who are present in each Light-Channel therapy session. The healing success "happens" by allowing it to happen in the service of the all-encompassing light. The objective of the therapy is to dissolve blockages in the flowing light channel so that the light can once again supply all of the cells in the body with the life force.

The holistic perspective of my therapy is not just directed at the individual organs and parts of the body. Instead, it supplies the entire body *and soul* with an inconceivable, intelligent light force. Light-channel work has a stimulating effect on the flow of the energy system and harmonizes *all* of our energy. This results in a good basis for the self-healing power of the body. The basic knowledge about the energy system should be accessible to every human being since it is precisely this system that is responsible for providing all of the organs and body cells with light and the life force. This will be explained in greater detail in the following sections.

Our body's energy system is subject to a higher intelligence—heavenly forces that manifest the eternal laws of light down to the smallest cells of the body. Cosmic light waves flow through the body in a balanced system of light channels. All of life thrives because of the light; it streams, flows, and moves. Our body remains healthy, alive, and filled with the life force because of the invisible light waves, and every organ, every cell of the body acts in accordance with the high laws of the creative intelligence. The invisible light flows around the body as a rainbow-colored aura. It nourishes the body with the light and life force, promoting its physical and emotional well-being.

However, when the cosmic light can no longer flow freely, the emotional state darkens and the body suffers from fatigue and exhaustion—a lack of life force. We no longer feel in harmony with ourselves and our surroundings. Through the Light-Channel work, the body is retuned like an instrument that harmoniously adds its tone to the great cosmic orchestra. The light channels are the strings of the instrument. The entire cosmos is like a wonderfully sounding symphony, and every living being adds its tone to this powerful orchestral music. Being in harmony with the cosmic music means: having light, life force, joy, and peace flow through us. I call the light that flows through everything the *Cosmic Christ Light*. It unites the entire Creation within itself. It is the bearer of cosmic wisdom and intelligence. As a result, spiritual light and life force flow through our energy system in the physical body to keep it healthy and also keep our soul in good spirits. Light-Channel therapy can also be effective in the emotional area by releasing or transforming painful feeling such as fear, sadness, disappointment, anger, and rejection. In this fundamental state of being filled with light, the body and soul can never be seen separately from each other. Instead, the body is the instrument of the soul's emotional state. It expresses the inner state.

Health disorders arise when there are blockages in the energy system—obstructions that disturb the gentle flow of the life force. This causes not only the body to suffer but also affects the soul. A sensitive touch by the hands can dissolve such disruptive fields and release blockages in the flowing energy system. This promotes the powers of self-healing and frequently brings such a lasting improvement of well-being that the respective individual feels that a small miracle has occurred. With this new therapy, I have been able to help countless people become free of chronic afflictions and pains that had mostly been treated unsuccessfully. This book also demonstrates how we can also stimulate the flow of life force within ourselves and others for the purpose of holistic healing.

Opening the light channel has never been as important and indispensable as today. On the one hand, a high degree of sensitivity is developing; on the other hand, many people are forced to constantly expose themselves to the blocking electromagnetic disruptive fields that are produced by computers and modern communication technology. The air and the ether are full of waves and disruptive fields that are harmful for human beings and nature to the same degree. Electrosmog from the atmosphere and various devices cause obstructions in the energy system, block the flow of the light and therefore greatly reduce the life force. This is where we find the true cause of the burnout syndrome. Many people suffer as a result from health disorders and states of exhaustion, frequently subjecting themselves to expensive examinations that show no findings on the organic level. Such widespread disorders of the body's energy supply can be successfully treated through Light-Channel Healing.

Yet, this therapy is not just a blessing for those who must do their daily work with computer monitors—it offers people of all age groups an outstanding possibility for increasing their well-being and freeing the energy system of blockages. Light-channel work also means an opening up to the spiritual light source. These inner connections are invisible openings to the spiritual dimension. The God-man Jesus lived in a state of intimate union with the Primal Light. The Bible tells of a wonderful healing in which he spoke the powerful word Ephatha. It means: "Be opened!" (Gospel of Mark, 7.34)

> "...AND THEY BROUGHT TO HIM A MAN WHO WAS DEAF AND HAD AN IMPEDIMENT IN HIS SPEECH; AND THEY BESOUGHT HIM TO LAY HIS HAND UPON HIM. AND TAKING HIM ASIDE FROM THE MULTITUDE PRIVATELY, HE PUT HIS FINGERS INTO HIS EARS, AND HE SPAT AND TOUCHED HIS TONGUE; AND LOOKING UP TO HEAVEN, HE SIGHED, AND SAID TO HIM, "EPHATHA," THAT IS, "BE OPENED." AND HIS EARS WERE OPENED, HIS TONGUE WAS RELEASED, AND HE SPOKE PLAINLY." (REVISED STANDARD VERSION OF THE BIBLE)

In summary: Through my many years of experiences as a holistic health practitioner, I have developed a system of Light-Channel work with which the entire energy system with its most important energy channels can be stimulated so that the vital energy can once again flow freely. This occurs in a sensitive, loving, and gentle way—and with the support of the healing angels. The hands are used to free the blocked zones of the disruptive energetic fields. The stimulated light energy from the fingertips and hand chakras is transmitted into the flowing energy system. The flowing of the conductive channels is activated, which has the effect of activating the overall energy circulation. Improving the supply of the life force to the body has a holistic effect: It frees us of both psychological and physical pain. Even though Light-Channel Healing is a distinctly gentle therapy, this in no way reduces its effectiveness. On the contrary—the rate of proven healing results has been absolutely astonishing.

AN EXAMPLE FROM MY PRACTICE

Here is the story of one of these astonishing cases of healing: A young woman was referred to me by her doctor. She suffered from intense disorders such as allergies and had circulatory collapses, cramps, and feet that would suddenly turn blue. None of the medical treatments achieved the desired degree of success. In her desperation, she went to a psychiatric clinic. Computer tomography was done, but the cause for her illness was not found. Neither medication nor any other approach helped her with these serious problems and disorders. She was unable to work for six months and did not know how her life would continue.

1st Treatment (February 16, 2000)

I found enormous blockages at the nape of her neck. Normally, there are corresponding emotions connected with such blockages. Since I did not perceive any feelings of fright or fear, I assumed that a major accident resulting in loss of consciousness could be the cause. When I asked her about it, she responded that she had suffered a major car accident 7 years earlier with internal injuries and that she had been unconscious. The solar-plexus chakra was completely empty and the six other chakras had to be newly integrated. The blockages at the nape of the neck dissolved during the treatment, and her entire energy circulation began to tingle like carbonation in a glass. She felt a strong current flowing through her.

2nd Treatment (March 22, 2000)

The young woman seemed very relaxed and felt much better. After so many unsuccessful treatments, she felt that this energy therapy had truly helped her. Her digestion is still weak, which means that she suffers from flatulence. There are still blockages in the head to be dissolved. So her entire energy system was thoroughly released once again.

We made another appointment for April. She called me beforehand and reported that she was feeling very well and did not need any more treatment! We were both very thankful for this result.

This is just one example of many. However, I would like to emphasize: The work on the light channels is not a substitute for conventional, scientific medicine! Yet, it closes a gap in the knowledge and understanding of the true causes of health disorders. Light-channel work creates the foundation for physical and emotional well-being. It is an urgently needed complement to scientific medicine. But it is not a substitute for it—and it also does not replace going to the doctor. Readers should continue to see the doctor or naturopath of their choice for health problems. The innovative Light-Channel work depicted in this book is a complementary method for activating the powers of self-healing. As a result, it has a preventative and supportive effect on the healing of diseases.

Fundamentals of Light-Channel Healing

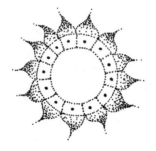

Yin and Yang
or the Law of Polarity

Yin and Yang

The ancient Chinese world view world was based on laws that apply equally to nature, the cosmos, and the human body. According to their understanding, the entire Creation consists of the two complementary basic forces of yin and yang. All life forms exist within the field of tension between these two different principles. Where there is light, there is also shadow. Yin means the shadow side of the mountain, yang the sunny side of the mountain. Both principles unite into a whole and strive to come together in harmony. This trinity is found in the smallest components, as well as in the expanses of the cosmos.

> YIN
> is condensing and its nature is dark, cold, feminine, and receptive.
>
> YANG
> is dissolving and its nature is light, warm, masculine, and flowing.
>
> CH'I or the life force
> is subtle electricity that flows between opposites or poles.

We usually perceive through differentiation: for example, the temperature is somewhere between the two extremes of heat and cold, a day between light and dark, the breath between in and out, and the emotions between love and hate, courage and fear, etc. Born as a man or as a woman, we embody these opposites and yet still unite both aspects within us.

Yin	Yang
Feminine	Masculine
Passive	Active
Night	Day
Moon	Sun
Cold	Heat
Winter	Summer
Shadow	Light
Earth	Heaven

Water is very suitable for illustrating the interplay of yin and yang because of its various aggregate states: In an extreme yin state (cold) it forms ice; in an extreme yang state (heat) it boils and turns into steam.

Like the human body, the entire planet Earth is subject to the law of yin and yang. During the day, the warming, radiating sun (yang) shines and the night is ruled by darkness and cold, with the moonlight (yin) reflecting the sun (yang). The four seasons also demonstrate this principle in an impressive way: In spring, after the spring equinox, the yang principle increases. It becomes warmer, nature begins to sprout and thrive under the light of the sun. Starting with the autumn equinox, the yin principle increases its influence more and more, and winter is completely in keeping with the yin principle—cold and barren. At the polar zones of the planet Earth, a barren, extreme yin state predominates; on the other hand, a barren, extreme yang state rules the hot deserts. This dramatically illustrates how growth and thriving can only occur when both forces are in harmony with each other! This principle applies to both the macrocosm and the microcosm, the human body.

The successful approach to health taken by Traditional Chinese Medicine consists of creating or maintaining precisely this harmony in the energy system of the human being. Disharmony between the two complementary basic forces of life is what produces disease. Thanks to the ancient Chinese, the extremely helpful knowledge about the meridians, this subtle energy system that transports the life force chi' through the body like a delicate electrical network and provides it with the necessary Light, is available to us. The life force flows throughout the entire body like a very gentle current and supplies all of the cells with energy. New life force is also continuously created from our food, the air we breathe, and our inherited dispositions. As far as I know, the wonderful laws of the Divine Creative Light are at work behind all of this.

Although the system of Light-Channel Healing that I have created is based upon the perceptions of the ancient Chinese teachings about meridians, no needles or other devices are required for the treatment, as I have already mentioned: Laying on hands is enough to stimulate and harmonize the current or the ch'i. I feel that the ch'i and the meridians are connected with the high vibration of the Christ Light. And this adds a new dimension to the traditional treatment of the meridians according to Traditional Chinese Medicine: It is the spiritual Light World of the healing angels. They serve the Christ Light and direct the currents of light through the body in this energy system. The Light Force is bestowed upon the practitioner through the connection to these high Light Beings, who are ready to help him. In the second section of this book, I suggest an attunement within the course of the therapy session that can open the consciousness to the spiritual Light World.

I will never forget a vision that showed me a new dimension of Light some years ago. Through my third eye, I saw a geometric grid of white Light that encompassed the entire universe. The connecting points of the joined corners consisted of triangular lines. In the middle of the global grid, a cross of golden Light was radiating. At the time, I was very moved by this vision, but I had no idea back then that a new dimension was being opened for us human beings. Now I am able to feel more and more that we are allowed to draw on this Light with our consciousness. Especially the meridians in our energy system are oriented upon this Light order. This is why I call this new method Light-Channel Healing. To me, genuine healing ultimately means a new orientation of the body and spirit within the cosmic order of the Christ Light. Higher organizing forces or angelic beings work as the mediators between Light and matter in this process.

Light-Channel Healing is also a very pleasant treatment. It has a soothing, relaxing effect and is extremely healing for emotional or physical problems through the loving, gentle laying of the hands on the meridian currents of the body. All methods of healing, including those of conventional medicine, should recognize that the true cause of health disorders is a disharmony in the energy system. There is no doubt that Light-Channel Healing will become an urgently needed complementary method of treatment in our health system. As a gentle revolution, it will also positively influence the skyrocketing costs of the health-care system.

THE THOUSANDS AND THOUSANDS OF BEINGS,
THE RECLINING YIN, IT SUPPORTS THEM,
THE MOVING YANG, IT SURROUNDS THEM.
THE ALL-EMBRACING LIFE FORCE
CREATES A HARMONIOUS UNISON.

LAO TSE

Basic Knowledge About the Light Body

PROTECT YOUR BODY AND
CONSIDER IT TO BE A
LIGHT-FILLED, WONDERFUL
SACRED SANCTUARY!
MESSAGE FROM THE ANGELS

The Subtle Body and the Material Body

With the physical sensory organs, we only perceive a limited spectrum of reality. We call this material vibrational plane the world of matter. The physical body has a material nature.

However, behind this visible plane is an invisible Light world that emerges out of the Divine Source of Light and works together with the material plane in a wonderful way. St. Hildegard of Bingen described a vision of rejoicing angel hierarchies and saw nine levels of various Light worlds with very specific tasks. In a mysterious way, we are in a constant state of exchange with the powers from the spiritual world with our consciousness—whether or not we even perceive it. Our subtle body is constantly bathed in this beautiful angelic Light. So we move in the midst of a luminous, invisible Light body, our aura, which surrounds us like a protective mantel of Light and penetrates the body. This flowing Light is our life force. The Light body is concealed from the physical eyes. However, it can be visibly measured through radiesthesia (dowsing or the use of the pendulum) and by clairvoyance, i.e. with the third eye. It forms a field of delicate rainbow-colored Light with a diameter of several yards around the physical body. So the truth is that we are much larger than we think!

The frequency of a human being is often perceived when he or she enters our aura—even when we do not see the person. Our energy fields then flow into each other. However, the energy field is not a closed system because everything in Creation is connected with everything else through the all-encompassing Christ Light. We can open our consciousness to this dimension, which permeates everything, with our consciousness when we succeed in achieving inner peace and immersing ourselves in the unity beyond time and space. Through daily meditation, the inner gifts will develop. The last section of this book discusses the development of the psychic abilities that slumber within all of us and wait to be cultivated. As if we are embedded in an immense radiant body, everything around us and within us is guided with infinite love and wisdom for us to blossom in this light of love.

The human being and the cosmos

Chakras or Light Vortexes

A gentle flooding of the body with Light and the life force occurs through the chakras. Seven major chakras provide the influx of cosmic Light and form delicate, colorful energy vortexes: Two of these centers are found on the head and five are distributed along the spinal column. The chakras draw the Cosmic Light into the body and are connected with the most important body glands. Chakras are the main openings for the Divine Light, and they reflect the entire spectrum of refraction, as is visible in the light of the rainbow. They are like opened petals in the Divine Light and shine on the invisible Tree of Life.

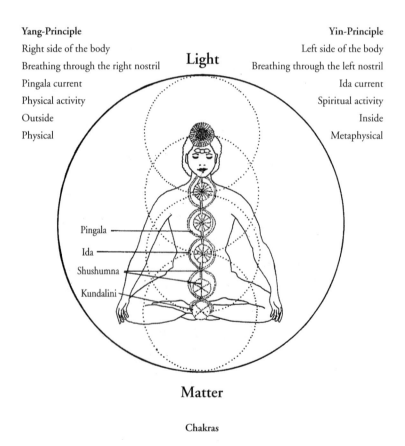

Yang-Principle

Right side of the body

Breathing through the right nostril

Pingala current

Physical activity

Outside

Physical

Light

Yin-Principle

Left side of the body

Breathing through the left nostril

Ida current

Spiritual activity

Inside

Metaphysical

Pingala

Ida

Shushumna

Kundalini

Matter

Chakras

As described in the practical instructions, the Light-Channel work includes the integration of the chakras into the cosmic Light current. Sometimes they turn in the wrong direction and, as a result, are like flowers that close at night. Consequently, the life force is considerably weakened. Through the Light-Channel work, the chakras are opened, balanced, and also freed from the disruptive fields of negative emotions.

The two energy currents *Ida* and *Pingala,* which spiral upward around the chakras of the spinal column in a snake-like manner, are related to the most fundamental yin-yang rhythm. *Ida* corresponds with the yin principle and the left side of the body, while *Pingala* corresponds with the yang principle and the right side of the body. The activated energy of *Ida* makes it possible for consciousness to open inwardly to the spiritual dimension, while that of *Pingala* allows it to open to the outside for physical activities. The central channel *Shushumna* follows the spinal column. When it flows, it opens to the dimension of Divine Light. This desired harmony was depicted as the Caduceus, the snake staff of Mercury, in earlier times and still serves as the symbol of the medical professions today.

The chakras reflect the spiritual growth of a human being in a refined raising of his or her frequency. We can achieve an increase of this frequency through a lifestyle that is based on spiritual values and goals and by brightening our state of mind through positive thinking and feeling. Meditation, especially the Lord's Prayer as a chakra meditation, has an enormous effect in refining and strengthening the flow of Light. The uppermost principle of our spiritual growth is always love.

Light Channels–
Energy Channels–
Meridians

In addition to the seven major chakras, we have twelve Light Channels or meridians, the course of which, as mentioned above, was shown by the ancient Chinese healing arts. As a flowing system—the energy circulating from the head to the feet, from the feet to the chest area and on through the arms to the fingers, and from the fingers to the head—they ensure the distribution of the life energy, the ch'i. The chakras draw Cosmic Light into the body. Then the energy channels distribute it through the delicate electrical network of the Light or life force to all of the body's cells and to all of the organs. Yin energy and yang energy flow as opposite-poled currents in the entire body and form a circulating system of flowing Light.

The body simultaneously has six yin channels and six yang channels—on the right and left side—for the Light flowing through it. From the feet to the chest region and down through the arms to the fingertips is how the *feminine* yin energy current flows; the *masculine* yang energy current flows from the fingertips up to the head and from the head down to the feet. The two main currents rule through these twelve Light channels, as depicted in the illustrations in the appendix.

Blockages must not obstruct the lively flow! The two power currents yin and yang should have a harmonious relationship with each other. Unfortunately, blockages frequently form in the channels, which immediately manifests as a disturbed sense of well-being and can lead to emotional and physical pain and disease. Precisely these blockages are the true causes of health disorders!

When the Light Channels are constricted or congested, the same thing happens as in an irrigation system when the flow of water is blocked somewhere or dammed up. Dammed water rises and the result is a flood. The amount of water on the one side of the obstacle is reduced

Meridians – Circulating Light Channels

(Only one side of the body is depicted here)

Yin-Energy	Yang-Energy	Yang-Energy	Yin-Energy
↓	↓	↓	↓
Flowing from the chest to the fingertips	Flowing from the fingers to the head	Flowing from the head to the feet	Flowing from the feet to the chest
↓	↓	↓	↓

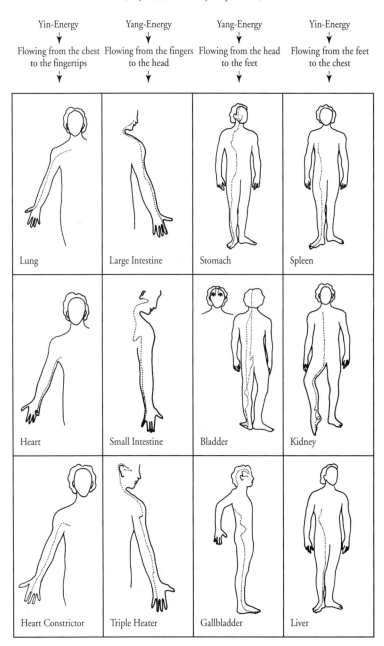

Lung	Large Intestine	Stomach	Spleen
Heart	Small Intestine	Bladder	Kidney
Heart Constrictor	Triple Heater	Gallbladder	Liver

in proportion to how much is dammed up on the other side. The same thing can occur within the body when the channels are blocked. As a result, certain parts of the body have too much while others have too little energy. The body and soul react with discomfort or pain to such disharmonies.

This treatment of the Light channels, which I have tested for many years, is a very effective method for releasing such blockages so that the body is once again provided with fresh life force. However, not just the body but also the soul is restored to health through the elimination of the energetic blockages. Enjoyment of life and cheerfulness are the energies of the Light and cannot be separated from the physical condition. Every sense of unease, every pain, every depressed bad mood, even every negative feeling is a blockage in the flowing current of life energy. An invisible, wonderful network connects the body with spiritual Light energy. The emotional and physical condition is inseparably interwoven with this flowing Light system, and blockages not only cause physical complaints but also darken the emotional state.

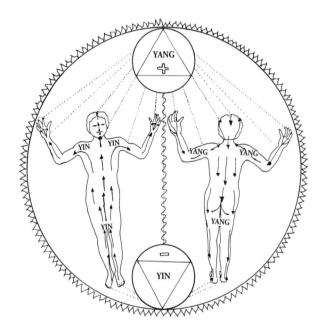

Yin and yang—currents of life

The human being and the tree

We have seen that the life force in the meridians circulates in a cycle. This is similar to a tree, whereby our hands can be compared with the branches and leaves of a tree that absorbs the sunlight. From each of the hands, three yang Light currents stream through the arms to the head. From here, the life force is directed into three other yang channels and transported down to the feet on both sides of the body. Like the roots of a tree draw water and nutrient salts from the ground and transport it upward through osmosis, the human being absorbs yin energy from the ground. From the feet, three yin channels flow through the legs up to the chest. In the chest area, three more yin energy channels pick up the current of Light and send it into the fingertips. This is where the energy system comes full circle. The continuous flowing in these twelve Light Channels provides the body with an absolutely intelligent life force that knows precisely how to keep the body alive and functioning well. The energy and life force circulating in this manner is brought into all of the cells, organs, and body parts.

Through the Light-Channel treatment that we give others, we can also learn to become more aware of own body, feel the energy system, and activate the life currents. In this way, a great deal can be contributed to living a fulfilled life. We enjoy better health—and this at a minimal cost and through our own personal responsibility! Streaming Light positively transforms the emotional and the physical condition—and this applies equally to ourselves and others. The third section of this book provides some helpful advice for using the Light-Channel treatment on ourselves.

Causes of Blockages in the Meridians

GO INTO THE STILLNESS, BELOVED SOUL!
HEAR THE BREATH OF GOD
FLOWING THROUGH YOU
LIKE A GENTLE BREEZE.

MESSAGE FROM THE ANGELS

So what are these outer and inner influences that continuously act upon the flowing energy system?

EMOTIONAL CAUSES

Thoughts and feelings influence the life force. Here is a brief summary of the subtle correlations of emotions and the life energy:

> *Fury* and *anger* move the life force upward
>
> *Worries* and *concerns* congest the life force
>
> *Mourning* and *melancholy* exhaust the life force
>
> *Fear* makes the life force sink downward
>
> *Joy* to an excessive degree scatters the life force

Especially the organs *heart* and *liver* react very sensitively to strong emotions!

When a person's head turns red and the veins on his or her temples swell, this is an unmistakable sign of anger: We see how the life force moves upward as a result. Frequently, after the death of a beloved partner, the other partner will also follow within a short period of time because deep mourning has exhausted his or her life force. An event that produces fright and fear can lead to incontinence (uncontrolled release of urine) because the life force sinks downward. An extremely effusive joy could trigger a sudden cardiac arrest because the life force has been too strongly scattered.

From this perspective, it is obvious that the life energy is intimately connected with the emotional condition. Flowing life energy corresponds with the principle of love. Blockages darken the Light and weaken the life force.

Growth and development toward the Light require an attentive observation of our own thoughts. Thoughts and imagination are creative forces, and life is largely oriented upon them. They form resonance fields in the aura and attract whatever was nourished by the thoughts. Positive or negative feelings are produced depending on the thoughts. (More about this in the last section of the book.) However, the spiritual helpers act with inconceivable wisdom and bring us together with people who either reflect the contents of our own soul or who help us to further develop ourselves. Our emotional growth processes are often accompanied by suffering. Suffering purifies the soul or gives us the strength needed for making changes in our life.

Traumas are among the most significant causes of energy blockages and physical complaints. Accidents are frequently responsible for burdening the energy system and the chakras with emotions like fear, fright, or rejection. These are primarily those feelings whose pain was not experienced during an accident, shock, or other occurrences and were consequently stored as a disruptive field.

External Causes

Every day we are subjected not only to feelings, but also to outer influences. These are not just conflicts with fellow humans that we must face, but also the fact that we live with a multitude of *electrical devices* and *environments* that emit electromagnetic radiation. This radiation is often too strong for our own sensitive network of delicate electrical channels. It causes a constriction of our Light channels mainly in the area of the neck, the head, and the upper body. Such blockages can then disrupt the energy system in the entire body. They also separate us from the nourishing Light, from the Light world of the angels. The emotional condition becomes darkened, and the health of the body suffers as a result.

Scars can also have an intensely disruptive effect on the energy system. When scars disrupt the course of one or more channels because of an accident or an operation, blockages occur in the entire system.

Sometimes the causes of energy blockages can be found in disruptive geomantic zones, especially when the sleeping area is negatively affected. Computers should never be placed in the sleeping area.

Drugs, alcohol, or an unhealthy diet can also be the causes of energy blockages. It is obvious that every abuse of our health burdens our energy system.

Causes of blockages can also be:

> Emotional pain and stress, sorrow, anger and worries, negative thinking and feeling
>
> Emotional growth processes meant to purify the soul's Light
>
> Traumas, i.e. emotional shocks from the past that are stored in the energy system as fears, rejection, fright, grief, anger, or a sense of repulsion
>
> Electro-smog from the ether, from computers, cell phones, television sets, antennas, and all other electrical devices and wiring
>
> Environments that are not in unison with the cosmic harmony such as disruptive geomantic zones, water veins, and disharmonious workplaces
>
> Accidents, physical injuries, scars, and drugs
>
> The wrong diet and too little exercise outdoors

A physical feeling of unease and emotional suffering show that the energy system is no longer flooded with sufficient life-maintaining current of Light. After all, the suffering also has the purpose of making a correction so that the body and soul once again resonate according to the Cosmic Light order.

With Light-Channel work, we can make a positive contribution to the benefit of our fellow humans and ourselves. However, we should remember that the bigger picture of spiritual lessons and growth processes that are to be accomplished in a specific lifetime are not always clear to us. Still, we can humbly do whatever we can with the assistance of the healing angels.

>> **Flowing Light** creates well-being, enjoyment of life, and a healthy emotional and physical condition.

>>| **Blocked Light** creates feelings of unease, suffering, and pain in the emotional and physical condition.

It is important to be familiar with the basics of the meridian system so that we know the course of the six yin and the six yang meridians. This is enough for Light-Channel Healing. The reason is simple: Every Light-Channel treatment that is given in the sequence that I have tried, tested, and taught for many years stimulates the entire energy system and makes the life force flow. It has been demonstrated that detailed knowledge about the branches or acupuncture points of the meridians is not necessary for the success of the treatment. Most meridians have various branches going to the corresponding organs. However, for Light-Channel Therapy as described by the text and illustrations in this book, only the main currents need to be discussed. The appendix has illustrations with the more exact course of the meridians. (The Recommended Reading section on page 156 also contains books with additional information).

Flowing Light–Blocked Light

FLOWING LIGHT = POSITIVE FORCES

BLOCKED LIGHT = NEGATIVE FORCES

This table provides a summary of how negative qualities can be transformed into positive qualities through the Light-Channel work as the blockages in the corresponding meridians are dissolved. The outer circle shows the negative forces, and the positive forces are depicted in the inner circle. Feelings are subject to the cosmic Light Order, which is the purest love.

In addition, it illustrates the sequence of the energy circulating in the meridians in a clockwise direction.

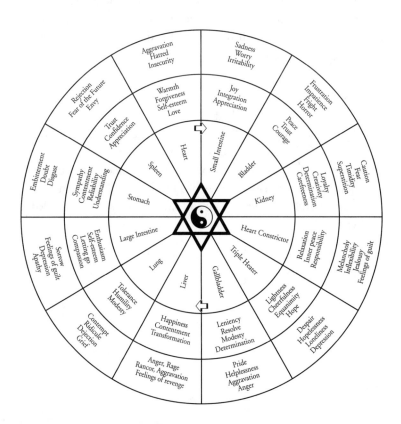

Blockages in the Meridians and Health Problems

The following two illustrations offer a summary of the correlations between specific disease patterns and Light Channels. The first illustration summarizes all of the yang meridians, and the second shows all of the yin meridians. The two main vessels—the Conception Vessel, which rules over all of the yin channels, and the Governor Vessel, which rules over all of the yang channels—are also depicted.

Just as Light-Channel Healing does not just treat the individual body organs or parts, diseases also cannot be cured through just one individual meridian. True healing occurs through an unimpeded flow of life force in the entire system. These healing currents of life energy, which make it possible for the body to be supplied with the Light and life force, give the body the strength to heal itself—through an improvement of the metabolism and hormonal activity and a strengthening of the immune system!

The course of a treatment as I have tested it over many years gives us the certainty that all of the Light Channels and all of the organs will be flooded anew with the life force during the treatment. With the knowledge of the flowing Light Channel system, we understand why a pain in the knee can very well be caused by a blockage in the neck or a headache can develop because of a blockage in the abdomen. It is important to study the illustrations and have a good working knowledge of them!

Healing Power through Light-Channel Healing
of Health Problems

6 Yang Energy Channels

with the Governor Vessel = Controller of All Yang Meridians

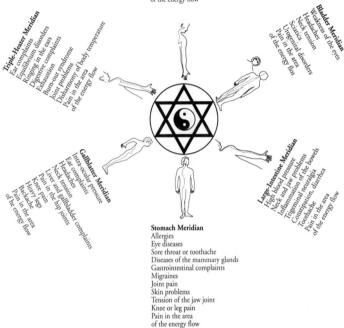

Small-Intestine Meridian
Digestive complaints
Problems in the jaw area
Ringing in the ears
Sense of numbness in the fingers
Neck tension
Pain in the area
of the energy flow

Bladder Meridian
Weakness of the eyes
Headaches
Neck tension
Sciatica
Urogenital disorders
Pain in the area
of the energy flow

Triple-Heater Meridian
Ear complaints
Equilibrium disorders
Ringing in the ears
Digestive complaints
Exhaustion
Burn-out syndrome
Joint problems
Disharmony of body temperature
Pain in the area
of the energy flow

Gallbladder Meridian
Intra-ocular pressure
Ear complaints
Headaches
Neck tension
Liver and gallbladder complaints
Pain in the hip joints
Knee pain
Heavy legs
Backache
Pain in the area
of the energy flow

Large-Intestine Meridian
High blood pressure
Neck and jaw problems
Inflammation of the bowels
Trigeminal neuralgia
Constipation, diarrhea
Toothache
Pain in the area
of the energy flow

Stomach Meridian
Allergies
Eye diseases
Sore throat or toothache
Diseases of the mammary glands
Gastrointestinal complaints
Migraines
Joint pain
Skin problems
Tension of the jaw joint
Knee or leg pain
Pain in the area
of the energy flow

Governor Vessel
Infectious diseases
Colds
Nosebleeding
Headaches
Backaches
Fatigue
Bronchitis
Nervous debility
Urogenital disorders
Pain in the area
of the energy flow

Healing Power through Light-Channel Healing for Health Problems

6 Yin Energy Channels

with the Conception Vessel = Controls All Yin Meridians

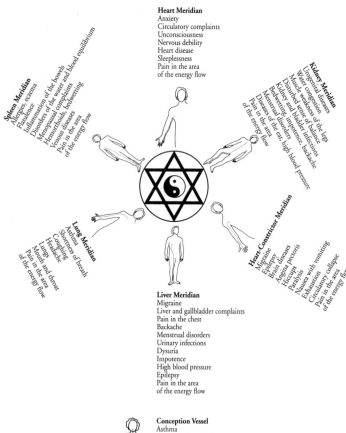

Heart Meridian
Anxiety
Circulatory complaints
Unconsciousness
Nervous debility
Heart disease
Sleeplessness
Pain in the area
of the energy flow

Kidney Meridian
Urogenital diseases
Water congestion of the legs
Muscle weakness of balance
Disturbed sense of balance
Kidney and bladder infections
Bedwetting, impotence, backache
Disease of the ear, high blood pressure
Menstrual disorders
Pain in the area
of the energy flow

Spleen Meridian
Allergies, eczema
Flatulence
Inflammation of the bowels
Disorders of the water and blood equilibrium
Menopausal complaints
Hemorrhoids, bedwetting
Venous diseases
Pain in the area
of the energy flow

Lung Meridian
Asthma
Shortness of breath
Coughing
Headache
Lungs
Mouth and throat
Pain in the area
of the energy flow

Heart-Constrictor Meridian
Migraine
Epilepsy
Brain diseases
Angina pectoris
Hiccups
Paralysis
Nausea with vomiting
Exhaustion
Circulatory collapse
Pain in the area
of the energy flow

Liver Meridian
Migraine
Liver and gallbladder complaints
Pain in the chest
Backache
Menstrual disorders
Urinary infections
Dysuria
Impotence
High blood pressure
Epilepsy
Pain in the area
of the energy flow

Conception Vessel
Asthma
Menopausal complaints
High blood pressure
Flatulence
Frigidity, impotence
Digestive problems
Speech impediments
Hoarseness
Urogenital problems
Heart-lung disorders
Pain in the area
of the energy flow

An Example from my Practice

Before we explore the actual process of Light-Channel work, here is another detailed example from my practice. In this regard, I would like to emphasize once again that I always give a complete treatment—no matter what the client's pain or problems may be. For me, the holistic human being is a holistic system of flowing life force. I always give a Light-Channel treatment as described in the practical section of the book.

1st Treatment

My client had been suffering from psoriasis of the scalp for many years. The skin was encrusted and the hair was only growing sparsely. In addition, she was suffering from a variety of allergies. Pollen and a great many different foods triggered vehement reactions. She was very aware of the pain in her left hip joint when she walked.

For years, she had tried many different therapies such as medications, ointments, homeopathy, bio-resonance, etc. None of these had brought relief from her serious problems.

The four lower chakras' polarity had to be reversed. The gallbladder meridian was heavily blocked on the left side of the body. This had a very negative influence on the hip joint. A strong blockage in the neck, connected with a feeling of rejection in the solar-plexus chakra indicated a trauma. I saw that something had happened during her school years. She told me that she was ridiculed at school on many occasions because she was overweight. I released the feeling of rejection from the solar-plexus chakra by gently touching the area of the blockage in the neck region with my fingertips until I felt it dissolve. As always, I did a complete Light-Channel treatment.

2nd Treatment (4 weeks after the 1st treatment)

The condition had improved enormously. However, my client did have a very strong period after the first treatment. The psoriasis on the scalp showed a noticeable improvement. Her energy was still quite blocked in the back. I released the coldness from her entire energy system. After the treatment, I suggested that she check back with me occasionally.

3rd Treatment (3 months after the 2nd treatment)

She was absolutely enthusiastic and said that these treatments were a true miracle for her. Her husband, who had been very skeptical, also could hardly believe it: no more psoriasis, no more pain in the hip joint. And the hair was growing back again on the scalp. She could once again eat everything without any problems. She wished that she had heard about my therapy at an earlier time. (I told her that I was in the process of writing a book to publicize the therapy.) She mentioned that she wanted to have a party to celebrate her healing.

I once again released her entire energy system, including all of the blockages that I found in the Light Channels. The Light had unfolded incredibly. With my third eye, I saw that it blazed in the most beautiful shades of blue and violet. Now she also saw these colors herself through her spiritual eye.

After this third and final Light-Channel session, we gratefully said goodbye to each other.

Light-Channel Healing

as

Therapy for Fellow Humans

A Few Words in Advance

> I GIVE YOU, BELOVED SOUL A BRIGHT LIGHT IN
> YOUR AURA SO THAT YOU WILL BE FULLY FILLED
> WITH THE LIFE FORCE.
>
> MESSAGE FROM THE ANGELS

Here is the practical approach to the Light-Channel Healing.

This is a step-by-step description of a Light-Channel treatment session. We can improve the physical and emotional well-being of our fellow humans considerably with these sessions: either within our own family and group of friends or as health practitioners with our own office, we can help relieve pain, activate the metabolism, and facilitate the healing of disorders and pain in the body and the soul.

Light-Channel work is a simple but effective therapy because—as mentioned at the beginning—it produces a pleasant stimulation and harmonization of the life force through gentle touch. An important precondition for this healing treatment is attention and love. This work requires us to have inner peace and time to dedicate to our fellow humans. An open heart chakra—the love center in the middle of our chest—gives us the empathy for and appreciation of those who are seeking our help. Flowing Light is the Light of love!

Our spiritual helpers, who know the plan for our lives, have possibly cultivated within us the desire to be there for other people and offer them help when they require it. Then we are being prepared for this wonderful work by the spiritual world: During a treatment, the rays of Light flowing out of our hands enter the energy channels of the person receiving the treatment in a gentle and releasing way. The Light and life force receive fresh impulses. Cosmic Light gives the body and soul life, and every atom resonates through this force. Love flows and streams. Love wants union. Love leads us back to the all-encompassing love. Healing energy dissolves all of the obstructions or blockages that impede the flow of the Light Channels.

Light-Channel Healing means placing ourselves in the service of all-encompassing love. This is a true spiritual task. The forces that are transmitted do not belong to the individual human being because only Divine Light is made up of the components that can produce tangible healing. This is why it is important to place great emphasis on our own emotional/spiritual development. The more we succeed in switching off our own will and becoming a channel for the influence of the spiritual Light World, the stronger the force coming out of our hands will be. Our vibration can be increased through daily meditation. We can use quiet prayers and invocations to connect with the intense radiance of the Light Beings that are present at every session supporting the flow of Light.

The last section of this book provides a detailed description of the essential steps for spiritual development. These steps support the awakening of new perceptions and insights about the invisible Light World, allowing us to discover dormant abilities of a spiritual nature within our own consciousness. Developing our own sensitivity is the only way for the gifts of clairsentience, clairaudience, and clairvoyance within us to unfold.

Now on to the practice!

The Treatment Room

Light-Channel therapy can actually be done in any peaceful place where there is a lounge (a bed or comfortable deck chair will also work if necessary). However, for those who plan to work with this wonderful energy therapy more frequently, it is better to set up a bright room with a pleasant temperature especially for the treatments. Then it is best to have a comfortable stool or chair without armrests and preferably a massage table. A second stool can be placed at the head and foot end for the practitioner. It is important that the client can lie down comfortably and that the work be done in a calm setting without any strain on the person providing the treatment. (For the sake of simplicity, the person receiving the treatment—no matter if this is a member of the family a man, woman, or even a child, will be called "the client" in the following.) The room should be lovingly decorated because the spiritual helpers will enjoy it and feel at home in the beautiful environment that we have prepared!

We receive our clients with a polite and friendly attitude, greeting them like guests. A friendly conversation that creates a harmonious mood sets the tone for each Light-Channel session.

The Treatment

The following 14 steps provide a summary of the Light-Channel treatment process. As mentioned above, the word "client" is used throughout the book for the person to be treated, but this term is obviously not limited to therapy within the scope of a holistic health practice. The mighty oak grows from the tiny acorn, so it is best for the Light-Channel therapy to initially be performed as wonderful healing support within the family or a group of friends! The client remains dressed for the treatment, but shoes should be removed and any tight belts must be loosened. The normal length of a Light-Channel session is between 60 and 90 minutes, depending upon the condition of the client.

Summary

THE CLIENT IS SEATED

1. Gently touch and tune into the shoulder-nape area
2. Release the entire spinal column from top to bottom
3. Smooth out the spinal column and once again lightly massage the nape of the neck

THE CLIENT LIES ON HIS/HER BACK

4. Balance the aura and the chakras *(standing at the side)*
5. Release the nape, neck, and back of the head *(standing or at the top of the head)*
6. Release the entire forehead area
7. Release the head points at the root of the nose, cheeks, and chin area
8. Release the sides of the neck and the collarbone to the shoulders
9. Release the upper arms and shoulder joints
10. Close the aura above the head

11. Smooth out the arms and release the finger points *(standing at the side)*

12. Release the knees and lower legs
    (standing or sitting at the feet)

13. Open ankle joints and feet

14. Give thanks and conclude

The Process in Detail

ATTUNEMENT

The client sits on a comfortable stool with his or her back easily accessible. The releasing of the energetic blockages begins with an attunement.

Place your hands very gently—without pressure—on your client's shoulders. Let your own thoughts turn into a willingness to let things happen and allow more space for your feelings. A brief attunement is soothing and calming. Use something like the following words (of course, they can be shortened or changed to fit the situation) to put yourself and your client in a harmonious, peaceful vibration:

"We will now become calm and have time for each other. To give more space to the inner peace, we pay attention to the flow of our breath and the feeling of how the breath very calmly flows in and out. Now we feel our feet on the ground. They are warm and wide. We feel the subtle roots that connect us with the depths of the Earth. The power of the Earth flows upward as yin energy from the feet through the legs. The pelvis is wide and relaxed.

We can imagine that a wonderful, radiant sun is shining above us. The Light flows over us and through us. Every cell of the body absorbs the healing Light of love. The Light current flows over the head–over the shoulders–over the arms and hands–over the back–over the belly–over the hips–and the legs–down to the feet. This wonderful healing Light pours into all of the chakras. We are tenderly wrapped in a protective cloak of Light and love. Light and healing power flow into all of our organs, into every part of the body. Each molecule, each atom is renewed or re-programmed. Energy flows from the head to the feet and from the feet to the head.

Everything that opposes the cosmic Light will now be released through the power that flows from my hands. I ask for the support of our spiritual Light beings so that this soul is refreshed with joy and this body with a renewed life force."

Depending upon the physical or emotional disharmonies, a corresponding affirmation can be added to this. As stated above, this attunement can be adapted or shortened using your own words. It is important to create a confidence-inspiring space, and the vibration of consciousness is increased through inner collection and concentration.

1. THE SHOULDER-NECK AREA

Your hands gently touch both shoulders. The inner peace makes it possible for you to attune yourself completely to your client's frequency. You may even perceive his or her emotional and physical condition. This is a form of clairsentience that is called *empathy.* Your brain waves will begin to resonate harmoniously with those of the client.

The hands begin to feel and perceive energy blockages as hard knots in the tissue or even as a negative feeling. Put your fingers on the places that are longing for the flow of energy. Stimulate these places by very lightly making circles with the fingertips. Wait until the blocked energy begins to flow.

Be aware that fear sits in the nape of the neck! The neck area should be given special attention during Light-Channel treatments. Traumas, i.e. emotional shocks or injuries, accidents, or other shocks usually cause strong blockages in the energy system in the neck area, and true emotional healing takes place by releasing these blockages. Psychotherapy should definitely take advantage of this possibility. Perhaps it will even be part of the psychotherapy of the future to treat traumas in this manner—and not just with words. In relation to the

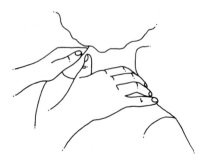

Releasing the neck area
Gently place your hands, without any
pressure on the client's shoulders.

shoulder and neck area, there is a detailed discussion of this important topic below.

This usually affects the *bladder meridian* that runs through the illustrated area, which is especially susceptible to emotional shocks becoming encapsulated as disruptive fields. These are the traumas that are trapped in the Light channel and can often date back to childhood—or even to the time of the mother's pregnancy. Usually these are fears, shocks, or feelings of rejection and disgust—negative feelings that occurred at an earlier time because of very specific events. The blockage lies in the meridian, but the related feeling is in the corresponding chakra, where it practically forms a dark cloud. These types of blockages can be the unrecognized source of considerable disruption for the emotional sense of well-being and the physical health if they are not treated

Here is a summary of the most frequently occurring feelings with the commonly affected chakras:

Fear, fright, panic	3rd or 4th Chakra
Rejection, criticism, feelings of disgust	2nd or 3rd Chakra
Loneliness, depression, helplessness	4th Chakra
Disappointment, mourning, self-criticism	4th Chakra
Concerns, pessimism, hatred	2nd or 3rd and 4th Chakra
Anger, aggravation, aggression	2nd or 3rd Chakra

In my many years of experience, Light-Channel work has proved to be an efficient, quickly effective form of psychotherapy. The painful feelings that obstruct the flow of energy can rarely be released through conversation alone. In order for true healing to occur, they must be released from the energy channels because they block the entire energy system and the chakras. Meridians and chakras form a unity that connects the body and the soul with each other.

If your client is experiencing intense emotions like fear or mourning, your inner guidance will use an image or symbol to show you when and where the emotional shock took place. Inner stillness and an expansion of consciousness will increasingly allow you to receive information and insights from the all-embracing plans of the cosmic Light. As in a dream, you will be able to "see" certain situations from childhood. This may sometimes just be an object or symbol that points to a traumatic experience. Speak carefully and sensitively about your "information" with the client and ask him or her what happened back then. Don't become discouraged if you haven't yet uncovered these abilities. With increasing sensitivity and practice, this "insight" will also be given to you.

Time and again, I am astonished when I see how certain negative events that we think have been long forgotten remain firmly rooted in the depths of the soul. They form false electrical fields and bind the energy to a negative feeling. The energy condenses and forms a disruptive field. The conscious memory of such events helps to free the corresponding meridian and chakra from the blockage, which is often perceived as a tingling—like the fizz that pearls upward in a glass of sparkling water—throughout the entire body. Frequently, there are also certain patterns that have already been experienced as a small child and repeat themselves time and again during the entire lifetime. The cosmic wisdom continuously shows us our own emotional state in the occurrences of everyday life—which is an opportunity for becoming conscious!

Light-Channel work—and particularly in the area of the shoulders and neck—frees the energy system of old emotional injuries. Precisely these emotions that are suppressed or hidden from consciousness are the true causes of health disorders. Then the actual experience, the *feeling* of the emotions has an enormous transformational effect. By experiencing them, these painful feelings are dissolved in the Light. A major sense of liberation is tangibly felt afterward.

Gently attune yourself with your client. In this empathetic manner, during the treatment you briefly feel what he is experiencing and carry the "cross," i.e. all of the suffering, of your fellow human being and free him of his emotional pain. Remember this: It is usually emotional pain that manifests in the body as a health disorder and waits for true "release"!

2. The Entire Spinal Column

After releasing the neck area, treat the entire spinal column from the neck downward to the coccyx (base of the spine). Lightly touch the spinal column with both thumbs. Place the rest of the fingers to the side of it on the back. Slowly work down the spinal column with the sense of feeling and releasing hardened knots. Two important energy currents are especially stimulated through the work on the back: the *bladder meridian* and the *gallbladder meridian.* When you gently touch these two energy channels, the energy begins to flow from the head to the feet. Lightly smooth out all of the vertebrae to the side. Let yourself be guided by your inner perception: The hands will feel drawn to the places that are longing to be flooded with energy.

3. Smoothing out the Spinal Column

After you have released the spinal column from the top to the bottom, smooth out the entire back two to three times from the top to the bottom. It is also helpful to visualize the entire back as a column of light and give the vertebrae enough space in your thoughts so that the entire back can expand! Briefly check to make sure that the neck has been released well enough. If necessary, you can give it more help by lightly circling with the fingers and massaging in the neck area.

After the back has been flooded anew with the life force, ask your client to lie down on the massage table. Cover the client snugly with a blanket and let him or her get comfortable on the table.

Releasing the spinal column
Treat the entire spinal column
from the neck down to the coccyx.

An alternative: It is also very possible to do the treatment in this position from the beginning if a client has problems sitting. If you start the treatment with the client on the table, first treat the aura and the chakras. Stand at the side of your reclining client to do this. Then move to the top of the head: While sitting or standing, place your hands gently under the shoulder blades and release the back from this position.

While standing on the right side of your (reclining) client, draw your healing hands slowly and attentively across the energy field of the chakras and the aura—from the neck to the feet. As you do this, hold your hands about 8 inches away from the body. Use the palms of your hands to perceive disharmonies of heat and cold in the aura and balance these.

When the life energy has been generally weakened through chronic diseases or depression, *a reversal of the chakra polarity* is often helpful. If you are familiar with the pendulum, you can use it to determine the state of the chakras. If it moves *clockwise,* this indicates that the chakra is open to the Cosmic Light. A *counterclockwise* movement means that the chakra is closed and the body is not permeated enough with Cosmic Light. Now the task is to reverse the polarity of the closed chakras. These chakras are like flowers closed at night that cannot absorb the sunlight. With the palm of your right hand, now circle in a clockwise direction in the aura above the base (root) chakra until you notice it opening. Hold the other hand above the next highest chakra. Also stay at a distance of about 8 inches from the body here.

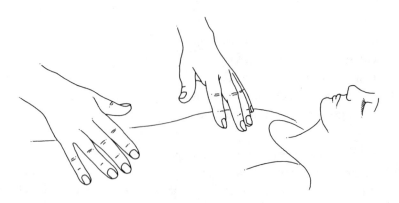

The energy field of the chakras and the aura
Slowly draw your hands across the energy field at a distance of about 8 inches from the body.

5. Releasing the Neck, Throat, and Back of the Head

Now move to the end of the table where the head is located. While either standing or sitting, put your hands under the neck and gently release the rest of the blockages in the back and side areas of the throat with lightly circling movements of your fingertips. The neck and throat are very important places in Light-Channel work!

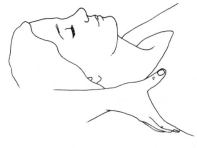

Hands beneath the neck
Put your hands under the neck and
gently release it.

Gently take the back of the head into your two hands that are open like a bowl. Blockages at the back of the head are often also the cause of sleep disorders and can additionally have a negative influence on the pituitary gland. Here, at the transition from the neck to the head, your sensitive touch as it releases the blocked energies is felt to be especially soothing. These areas have an analogy to the *pelvis:* Whatever is opened here also has a correlate in the pelvic region!

The following three channels, which are stimulated by the treatment, flow through the throat area from the hands and arms to the head: *triple heater – large-intestine meridian – small-intestine meridian.*

6. Releasing the Entire Forehead Region

The beginning points of the *stomach meridian* on the forehead at located at the hairline on both sides. Gently place your hands on the head and also on these points. Let the energy current begin to flow through your fingertips. Touching the two points stimulates the flow of this important channel with the organ of the stomach. When you touch the two frontal bumps, this is very stimulating for the *gallbladder meridian.*

Release the entire forehead region
Gently place your hands on the head
and on both sides at the beginning
points of the stomach meridian.

7. Releasing the Head Points at the Root of the Nose, Cheeks, and Chin Area

Close to the root of the nose, at the inner right and left corners of the eyes is the location of the beginning points of the *bladder meridian,* which runs over the head and down the back into the legs and the little toe from here.

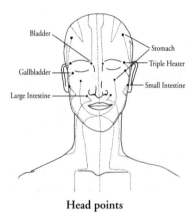

Bladder

Stomach

Triple Heater

Gallbladder

Small Intestine

Large Intestine

Head points

At the highest point of the cheekbones—to the side of both eyes—is the beginning point of the *gallbladder meridian.* These points just need to be touched gently. Circle them lightly and then let the energy currents flow.

The jaw joint also frequently displays strong blockages. Almost everyone who sits at the computer every day or frequently uses a cell phone for telephone conversations has these blockages. Tensions in the cheek area, which are also the cause of nightly grinding of the teeth, can lead to headaches or toothaches, among other things. Releasing the energy blockages in this area has a very relaxing effect. Afterward, release the chin through a gentle touch.

The following energy currents are stimulated on the face:

bladder meridian – gallbladder meridian – stomach meridian
triple heater – large-intestine meridian – small-intestine meridian

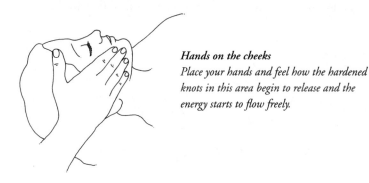

Hands on the cheeks
Place your hands and feel how the hardened knots in this area begin to release and the energy starts to flow freely.

8. Releasing the Neck at the Side and the Collarbone

Strong blockages often occur to the side of the throat, particularly in people who work long hours at the computer, spend much time watching television, or are exposed to other types of electrical disruptive fields. The *triple-heater meridian* reacts very sensitively to such disruptive fields. An energy weakness in this meridian, which is associated with the element of fire, can cause the so-called "burn-out syndrome." Without using any pressure, place your hands very carefully on the side of the neck beneath the ears until the energy congestion is released and the Light flows in.

Hands on the side of the neck
Without any pressure, place your hands very carefully on the side of the neck beneath the ears until the energy congestion is released and the Light flows in.

Now carefully release the blockages on the collarbone. The *stomach meridian* flows along the collarbone. Since this Light Channel influences everything that flows downward, this place is very important when energy is congested in the head. This type of disharmony can cause headaches, dizziness, or even stomach problems. Another possibility may be pain in the legs, knees, or feet when the energy cannot flow freely downward. Lay your hands here and feel how the hardened knots in this area begin to release and the energy starts to flow freely.

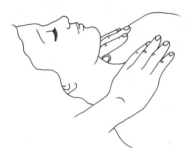

Hands on the collarbone
Now carefully release the blockages on the collarbone.

9. Releasing the Upper Arms and Shoulder Joints

Release the upper arms and shoulder joints by letting your hands rest for a while on the corresponding areas until the energy begins to flow. Some people suffer from pain in the shoulder joints, which form an analogy to the hip joints. It feels very soothing to have the shoulder joints touched and creates a strong energy flow because six different Light Channels are stimulated or activated!

At this point, I would like to add a few basic rules that invite you to take a holistic approach to the flowing energy system. Certain parts of the body have a particularly close relationship to other parts. I call these relationships *analogies* or correlates. During my treatments, I often feel that certain parts of the body are attuned to each other. In this way, the energy flooding of various body parts can occur at the same time. The following table shows the connection of different body parts with each other through analogies and how they can be treated on various levels. My next book will go into greater detail on this topic.

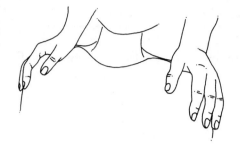

Releasing the upper arms and shoulder joints
Rest your hands for a while on the corresponding areas until the energy begins to flow.

ANALOGIES OR CORRELATES IN BODY AREAS:

Neck and back of the head → Pelvis

Head → Knee

Jaw joint → Side of knee joint

Shoulder joint → Hip joint

Wrist → Ankle

Head → Feet → Hands

Ankle → Neck and throat area

Shoulder blades → Bones to the side of the hips

I have observed these through the years and integrated them into my work—so try it out! You will be surprised by the results.

The organs have their correlates in the body openings on the head. A deficiency of life energy in these organs can manifest as complaints in the head area.

OPENINGS OF THE ORGANS LOCATED ON THE HEAD:

Kidney → Ears

Liver → Eyes

Stomach → Mouth

Spleen → Lips

Lungs → Nose

After you have released the head area, it is a good idea to close the aura above the head. With an attitude of contemplation, now move both hands from the neck over the face to above the crown chakra three times at a distance of about 4 inches. This makes the aura above the head area balanced and radiant.

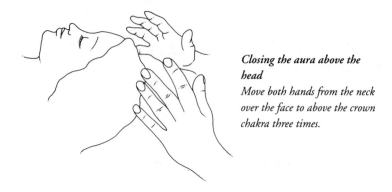

Closing the aura above the head
Move both hands from the neck over the face to above the crown chakra three times.

If you are already intuitive, bright Light bursting from the third eye will often show you that the energy channels are once again open to the Cosmic Light! Blocked energy is dark; the healing Light currents make the aura more radiant and bright. This is usually followed by a clear violet as healing energy and a soothing vibration. I like to interpret the violet ray of Light as the Light of Archangel *Raphael,* God's healing angel.

11. SMOOTHING OUT THE ARMS AND RELEASING THE FINGER POINTS

Next, very lightly smooth out the right arm on the inner side—with the three yin channels—from the shoulders to the palm of the hand.

Three Light channels with yin energy flow from the chest area through the shoulders to the fingertips on the inner side of the arms. They are the three Light channels with the corresponding organs:

Lung – heart constrictor – heart

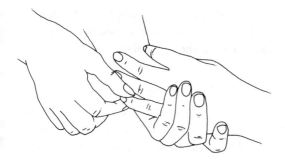

Now take the individual fingertips by the nail bed between your thumb and index finger. Circle to the sides of the nail bed for a brief moment. This releases the *ting points,* which are the beginning and ending points of the energy channels*. These important points have a soothing influence on the digestion, the blood-circulation system, and the entire energy circulation. At the same time, the gentle circling stimulates the corresponding organs:

On the nail bed of the thumb	→ Lungs
of the index finger	→ Large Intestine
of the middle finger	→ Heart Constrictor
of the ring finger	→ Triple Heater = heat regulation
of the little finger's inner side	→ Heart
of the little finger's outer side	→ Small Intestine

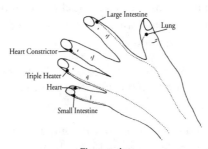

Finger points

* My most recent experience has shown me that these points provide important impulses for the Light Channels. This is why I now call them "Light-impulse points."

For this type of releasing, it is not that important to know which side of the nail bed the point lies because both sides are stimulated at the same time when it is held by grasping the fingertip with the index finger and thumb on both sides at the same time.

Now lightly smooth out the outer side of the arm—with the three yang channels—upward from the hands to the shoulder joint. Currents of the three Light Channels with yang energy run from the fingertips to the face on the outer side of the arm. These are the energy channels with the corresponding organs:

large intestine – triple heater – small intestine

The *triple heater* does not have a specific organ. However, it is very important for the heat regulation of the body. In addition, it rules the evaporation process of the lungs, the digestive juices in the upper area of the abdomen, and the digestive areas of the lower abdomen. It must provide these three very important levels with the element of fire. In terms of water circulation, it has the same function for the body as the sun does for the Earth.

Then change sides and move to the opposite area of the table. As before with the right arm, now release the finger points of the left hand by first smoothing out the inner and then the outer side of the arm.

12. RELEASING THE KNEES AND LOWER LEGS

Now move to the foot end of the massage table. Completing our Light-Channel session in a harmonious way, we always treat the legs and feet last. This is where we can harmonize the entire circulation of the energy channels from the head to the feet.

As you stand, carefully grasp both of your client's knees with your hands, placing the thumb on the inner side of the knee and the fingers on the outer side.

The knees are a good place to activate the entire circulation of yin and yang energy. The knee is correlated with the head and jaw area (see Point 9: Analogies, on page 57). From here, you can very effectively relieve and release headaches, dizziness, or toothaches.

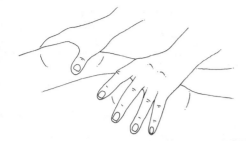

Releasing the knees
Through gentle touch,
feel and release the entire
shinbone from the knee to the
ankles.

Through gentle touch, feel and release the entire shinbone from the knees to the ankles. The *stomach meridian* flows along the outer side of the shinbones.

The *gallbladder meridian* flows on the outer side of the legs. Be sure to memorize the course of these two important channels or look at the illustrations in the appendix.

13. Opening the Ankle Joints and Feet

While standing or sitting, now grasp both ankles at the same time with your hands. As you do this, place your thumb on the inner side and the other fingers on the outer side. Gently hold the ankles until the energy begins to flow. The malleoli are very closely connected with the back of the head so that any remaining blockages at the back of the head can now be released. The remaining blockages of the head, chest, and abdomen can also be released on the upper side of the feet. As with the fingertips, the *ting points,* meaning the beginning and ending points of the meridians, are released on the nail beds of all the toes:

Ting points on the toes
The remaining blockages of the
head, chest, and abdomen can also
be released on the upper side of the
feet.

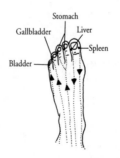

Stomach

Gallbladder   Liver

Spleen

Bladder

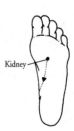

Kidney

On the big toe	→ Spleen
On the big toe	→ Liver
On the next two toes	→ Stomach
On the fourth toe	→ Gallbladder
On the little toe	→ Bladder
In the middle of the foot	→ Kidney

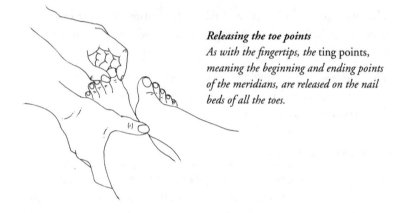

Releasing the toe points
As with the fingertips, the ting points, meaning the beginning and ending points of the meridians, are released on the nail beds of all the toes.

Now gently place your hands on the outer edges of both feet and hold both heels for a while. Feel how the two Light Channels associated with the element of water, those of the *kidney* and the *bladder* are stimulated and opened. This touch is very soothing for the draining organs and the entire energy flow from the head down the back and to the feet.

Releasing the heels
Now gently place your hands on the outer edges of both feet and hold both heels for a while.

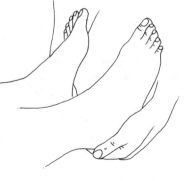

Lightly feel the entire foot. All of the hardened knots in the energy channels can be released in this way. Knowledge about the foot reflexology points is helpful, but not absolutely necessary. Now also release the metatarsophalangael joints (at the base of the toes). Depending on the client's condition, certain areas may be treated more intensively than others.

In conclusion, place your fingertips gently in the middle of the sole of the foot. This stimulates the beginning point of the *kidney channel,* which has the beautiful name of "Bubbling Spring." At the same time, this touch opens the chakras on the soles of the feet and the solar-plexus chakra.

By working on the feet, the following three Light Channels with yin energy, which flow from bottom to top, and the corresponding organs are stimulated:

kidney – liver – spleen

The three Light Channels with yang energy, which flow from the head to the feet, and the corresponding organs are stimulated:

bladder – stomach – gallbladder

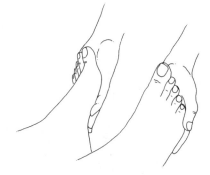

Releasing the middle of the feet
In conclusion, place your fingertips gently in the middle of the sole of the foot.

A silent prayer in gratitude for the invigorating healing power that we receive from the divine source of all life completes this wonderful Light-Channel work for every treatment. The certainty that giving is actually receiving will continue to grow stronger within you! You might even receive a message from the healing angels that you can pass on to your client. Some of these comforting messages from the angels are recorded here in this book.

Gently press the client's feet to let him or her know that the treatment is over now. Give him or her a few more minutes of quiet. Then have a brief conversation about how he or she now feels.

Practical Experiences

Since this treatment has a lasting and deep effect, you and your client should allow three weeks to pass before repeating the therapy. The body will gradually regenerate because of the new energy flowing through it. Of course, if there are vehement complaints, the treatment can also be repeated in shorter intervals. How often the treatments should be done depends on the client's own evaluation of his or her needs.

Through this deep treatment, the body and soul are filled anew with the life force. Reactions may also occasionally occur that are similar to those of the homeopathic remedies, which means an initial worsening. However, I have rarely observed such a response. Sometimes the body needs time to adapt to a renewed metabolism, but it has received the necessary strength through the Light-Channel treatment to regenerate and heal itself. As a rule, the client immediately feels refreshed, lighter, and often like reborn!

AN EXAMPLE FROM MY PRACTICE

Here is a description of an example from my practice. It is solely meant to show the possibilities of Light-Channel work that are available as you become increasingly sensitive and gain experience with it. Yet, even without clairsentience, you can do much good for your fellow human beings because the healing angels are always working with you!

1st Treatment

A 35-year-old woman came for her initial Light-Channel treatment. She suffered from pain, sleeplessness, and rashes. The medical diagnosis was soft-tissue rheumatism with psychosomatic disorders. She had tried out every possible medication and couldn't tolerate many of them, sometimes reacting with vomiting. Even a three-week stay at a health resort did not provide any relief from her pain. She was in despair and the doctor continued to prescribe new medications, which eventually also included anti-depressants.

During the first treatment, I perceived a strong blockage in the bladder meridian at the back of the neck, connected with a vehement feeling of fright in her heart chakra. I asked her during the treatment whether she had been involved in an accident. She told me about a serious car accident some years before. I kept my hand on blocked area of the neck until the fright in the heart chakra was released. In addition, a sense of helplessness and lack of self-esteem also overshadowed the heart chakra. I "saw" a relevant scene when she was at school. She remembered how much she had suffered during her school years because of the strictness of a teacher. This trauma was also released from her heart chakra.

Strong blockages obstruct the energy flow in the throat, the jaw, and the neck. Heat becomes congested in the upper body (the rash on her upper chest).

The stimulation of the Light Channels resulted in a beautiful unfolding of the Light.

2nd Treatment
There was a period of about four weeks between the first treatment and every additional treatment.

The client felt better, but in the meantime had experienced problems and also contracted an intestinal disorder during her vacation in northern Africa.

During this treatment, I felt an additional blockage in the neck area, connected with a sense of vehement rejection in the solar-plexus chakra. I "saw" how she was pulled by hands and forced–against vigorous resistance—to go into a house. I asked her if she had had this kind of experience. She remembered how, during her childhood, she once was forced to go to the dentist despite her intensive resistance. This strong sense of rejection had remained in her solar plexus.

The life energy was blocked in her channels. I released the sense of anger from her solar-plexus chakra. She confirmed that this feeling had been caused by conflicts with the neighbors.

Then I supported the release of all the Light Channels and the harmonization of her entire system.

3rd Treatment
The lower five chakras were turning in the wrong direction and had shut down. This had weakened the energy in her entire metabolic process.

I helped integrate the chakras by changing the direction in which they were turning. Her ears were under pressure. The energy was weak in her kidneys. The client was experiencing many problems at work.

I helped bring her entire energy system back into a state of flow.

4th Treatment

Her physical and emotional state had greatly improved. She no longer suffered from rheumatic pain and felt much better. She occasionally still had a slight rash on a certain part of the neck.

She still had some blockages in the neck and head. Since she worked at the computer, these blockages can manifest over and over again. During the treatment, I again felt a blockage in the bladder meridian at the neck, linked with a fearful feeling in the solar-plexus chakra. I "saw" her as a small child in a blossoming meadow, but had the feeling that she was stung by insects. She confirmed my impression and told me that she had fallen into an anthill at the age of 4 years and was badly "bitten." I released this old fear from her solar-plexus chakra.

During this fourth Light-Channel treatment, she was very happy that her third eye had opened and she was able to see the brightly luminous violet Light for the first time.

5th Treatment

The opening of the third eye had left a lasting impression on her. She was very glad that her condition had considerably improved. No more pain! Many months have passed since her last visit to the doctor and she feels wonderful. She is very thankful for these treatments.

During this fifth treatment, there was a very strong unfolding of the Light. While we were immersed in the Light, which I perceived with my third eye, I silently asked her Light Angel whether I was permitted to convey a message. At this moment, there was a slight crack in the wall behind me—a release of tension. I thought this was a wonderful sign! I asked my client whether she heard the crack. She had heard it and felt a delicate, sweet breath of air across her face at the same time. This experience made a strong impression on her. So we happily said goodbye to each other. She knows she can return if she needs any additional treatments.

Light-Channel Healing for Yourself

Awareness of Your Own Body

RECOGNIZE AND VALUE YOUR
UNIQUENESS. LISTEN WITHIN!
ONLY YOU ALONE KNOW YOUR
INNER TRUTH.

MESSAGE FROM THE ANGELS

You now have a fundamental knowledge about the laws of the life energy and have learned how to give a Light-Channel treatment to another person. This section will show how you can also open your own Light Channels and free them of blockages. You will be increasingly capable of feeling your body in stillness and attentiveness. Sense the fine currents of the life energy within your own body! As a result, you can start to mentally sense the blockages and release them. Please carefully observe the condition of your body. After all, it is a wonderful instrument for the soul and is filled with Light and power. But it is also a replica of the entire Earth—even the whole universe!

Begin by perceiving your body temperature. A balanced body temperature depends on a harmonious flow of the Light into the meridians as yin and yang energy. Yang is warm energy and yin is cold energy. Are your hands or feet cold? Cold feet mean stagnating yin energy from the ground or a lack of warming yang from the head. If you direct your consciousness into your feet, the energy will collect there because it follows your attention. The energy will begin to flow, and the feet can be warmed in this way.

Now try to perceive your energy blockages. Does your neck feel stiff or hardened? Is the back of your head blocked and the head too hot? In complete silence, take a very conscious look at all those places that need stimulation. It may take a few minutes for you to get the energy moving. In this manner, you will soon feel how the energy in your Light Channels obeys your mental powers, which are Light energy.

How does your neck and chest feel? Do you sense a dull, heavy burden on your chest? Take a very quiet look at the places that need to be flooded with energy. You will soon feel how the blocked energy also begins to flow here.

Pain is produced—as you can always best perceive in yourself—by a disharmony of the energy flow. This indicates that there are blocked areas in the Light Channels! It is very helpful to take an attentive look at the painful areas and accept the pain. The blocked energy will begin to move as a result of this attentive observation—as a result of the Light-filled power of the mind connected with the Light of the angels.

This is *one* possibility for removing blockages. The second possibility is: gentle touching of specific body areas. This has a more intensive effect. It is easy to learn the following methods of stimulating the Light channels. These sections explain how you can open your own Light Channels. This approach will help you make a great contribution toward a flooding of your own body with Light—as well as integrating yourself into the cosmic order of the Christ Light.

The Fingertips

A very good place to stimulate the flow of your own life energy is at the beginning and ending points of the Light Channels, the *ting points*. On the fingertips to the side of the nail bed—as described in the second section—you will find the beginning points of the three yang and ending points of the three yin channels. The yin energy flows from the ground upward to the fingertips, and the yang energy flows from the fingertips to the head.

Stimulate these important points with gentle pressure for about two minutes. When you do this, first circle the points lightly and then let the touch become a quiet sense of allowing the current to flow.

Releasing the fingertips

Stimulate the points illustrated in the sketch between your index finger and thumb. The entire energy system, especially the digestive and circulatory systems, will be filled with new strength by such gently touching the fingertips in this way. Light-Channel Healing also develops its outstanding curative powers here.

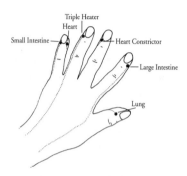

Ting points on the fingertips

The *lung meridian* (yin) ends at the thumb and changes into the *large-intestine meridian* (yang) at the index finger. Together they form a pair and are associated with the element of *metal* (air).

The *heart-constrictor meridian* (yin) ends at the middle finger and sends the energy to the *triple heater* (yang) on the ring finger. These two channels form a pair and are subject to the element of *fire.*

The *heart meridian* (yin) ends at the inner nail bed of the little finger and sends the energy to the *small-intestine meridian* (yang) on the outer side. Both meridians form a pair and are subject to the element of *fire.*

The *lung meridian*, which ends at the thumb, is responsible for the respiratory organs, as well as the energy supply for the Light Channel in the chest, arm, and thumb. From here, you can treat bronchitis, coughing, and colds.

Stimulating the beginning points of the *large-intestine meridian* on the index finger can bring relief in cases of sluggish digestion and constipation. Pain in your shoulder or arm can be released from here if there is a blockage in this channel.

When you stimulate the ending points of the *heart-constrictor meridian* on the middle finger, this harmonizes your peripheral circulatory system and distributes the life energy from the head down into the pelvis.

Stimulating the beginning points of the *triple-heater meridian* on the ring finger releases blockages in the upper arm, shoulder area, and the side of the throat area up to the ear. This important energy channel rules three levels: the lung area, the upper digestive organs, and the lower digestive level. The *triple heater* has an effect on the human organism like that of the sun on the Earth. If this Light Channel loses its power, the effects in the body are like the sun no longer shining outside in nature. The life force and the enjoyment of life disappear. The metabolism in the digestive tract is weakened. A deficiency of this warming fire can have a negative impact on the joints, the digestive system, a balanced body temperature, and the psyche, especially in terms of the enjoyment of life. The Light Channel of the *triple heater* reacts with heightened sensitivity to electro-magnetic radiation from computers and cell phones. These devices can, as mentioned above, cause immense blockages in the jaw area and in the side of the throat area. Light-Channel therapy offers you a welcome and very simple possibility of releasing the blockages created as a result of stressful working conditions by treating, for example, the beginning points of the *triple-heater meridian* on your ring finger time and again.

Touching and gently stimulating the little finger (ending point of the *heart meridian* and beginning point of the *small-intestine meridian)* brings the life force into your heart and the digestive area of the small intestine.

Not only do the heart and the digestion react outstandingly to a stimulation of the little finger, but also the entire area of the meridians' energy flow: The hand, the arms, the shoulders, and the neck are all freed of their energy blockages. This also applies to the other meridians: *All of the body parts receive the life force wherever the Light Channel flows through them.* Stimulating the little finger is also a very effective *first-aid point* for heart and circulatory disorders. This is a genuine **emergency point.** However, in case of such disorders always call a physician!

Stimulating the beginning and ending points of the channel in the energy system has an effect similar to flipping the switch in the electrical power network. Just a bit of pressure—and the light is on. A cord to the lamp makes this possible. The meridians are such cords. They provide the connected organs—comparable with luminous lamps—with the necessary life force. "Circuit-breaking" can also occur in our energy system. Light-Channel work eliminates such disruptive fields in the wonderful flowing system of the Light and power that surge through us.

Stimulation of the ting points makes possible a soothing and easily practiced opening of the Light Channels for yourself, as well as for people who are elderly or ill. This stimulation is especially helpful for children. You can combine the stimulating touch with a nursery rhyme—I have found this to be very fascinating for children. Women who are expecting a baby can have the complete Light-Channel work done on their fingers as a replacement for the other form of treatment!

The following is a summary of the physical and emotional complaints that can be healed through the Light work on the fingertips. As always, this applies to ongoing complaints: Consult a physician in whom you have confidence for clarification!

LIGHT-CHANNEL HEALING ON THE FINGERTIPS HAS A HEALING EFFECT FOR

> Physical complaints such as
> circulatory problems – heart complaints – headache – pain in fingers, arms, and shoulders – tinnitus (ringing in the ears) – dizziness – digestive problems – hot flashes – states of exhaustion – asthma – coughing – sore throat – sleeplessness

> Emotional problems such as
> States of anxiety – worries – sadness – feelings of guilt – inner unrest and feelings of tension – melancholy – depression – despair – pride – sarcasm – dejection

"Praying Hands"

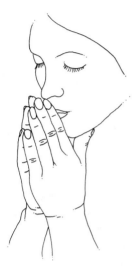

Putting your two hands together has a very subtle healing effect. The mystics of ancient times taught people to put their hands together for prayer. Putting the hands and fingertips together actually creates a strong flow of Light throughout the entire body!

Place the palms of your two hands together slowly and in an attitude of complete attentiveness. The two palms and the fingertips should touch each other lightly. A very special power is generated when—as shown in the illustration above—the folded hands gently touch the lips with the index fingers and the thumbs touch the chin. As a result of the soothing inner stillness as you rest in this position, you can perceive the healing currents throughout the entire body. If you now call out to your angels or spiritual helpers in silence, there will immediately be a connection to the higher dimensions of the Light. You will soon feel a beautiful, delicate flooding of Cosmic Light through the "praying hands." The hands create a strong energy field since the right side and left side are each poled differently. A highly sensitive power field is also generated around the lips.

When you gently touch the lower side of the chin, the blockages in the area of the salivary gland will be released. Blockages in this area can cause a constant stimulation of the salivary gland, which triggers a continual feeling of hunger. This is one of the major causes of overweight. Releasing the blockages in the chin area is the best and least expensive diet!

The following table has information about which complaints of a physical or emotional nature can be positively influenced with the position of the "praying hands."

LIGHT-CHANNEL HEALING THROUGH "PRAYING HANDS" HAS A HEALING EFFECT FOR

Physical complaints such as
headache – dizziness – high blood pressure – circulatory complaints – pain in the arms and shoulders – digestive complaints – stomachache – pressure on the ears and tinnitus (ringing in the ears) – heart complaints – states of exhaustion – overweight

Emotional problems such as
Dejection – feelings of loneliness – jealousy – feelings of guilt – hypersensitivity – lack of self-confidence – feelings of hatred – depressive moods

Touching the Face

The sketch shows an overview of the beginning and ending points of the Light Channels in the facial area.

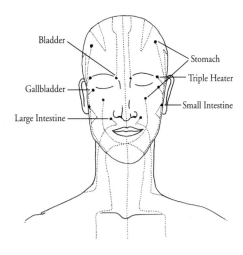

Head points

Imagine a tree! It has roots in the soil. The leaves open up to the sunlight. From the roots, the water with nutrient salts flows upward into each of the leaves and evaporates. The light of the sun is absorbed by the fine pores of the little leaves and transformed into matter. A cycle between above and below makes the tree into a provider of strength and life. Our fingers are similar to the branches of the tree, and our feet with their toes are like its roots. Strong energy fields are located at the fingertips and the toes. This is where yin energy changes into yang and yang energy changes into yin.

Yin energy also flows from the feet up to the chest and on through the arms into the fingertips. Yang energy flows from the fingertips along the arms to the head and down to the feet from there.

The following three yang meridians end at the face and begin at the fingertips:

> *Large-intestine meridian* along the side of the nostrils
>
> *Triple-heater meridian* at the temples
>
> *Small-intestine meridian* in front of the earlobes.

The face has three yang meridians that begin here and end at the tips of the toes:

> *Stomach meridian* over the forehead and beneath the eyes
>
> *Gallbladder meridian* at the highest point of the cheek
>
> *Bladder meridian* at the root of the nose near the eyebrows

With the following *touch,* you can learn to feel the Light Channels on the face and stimulate them. For about five minutes, place your thumbs on the lower side of the cheekbone (at the roots of the upper teeth) and the other fingers flat on the highest part of the forehead, as shown in the illustration.

Releasing the cheeks and forehead

This healing touch especially stimulates the *stomach meridian* and promotes the flow of life energy from the top to the bottom. You will soon perceive these delicate currents. This relaxes the entire head area, and you will feel lighter in the head and stronger in the belly and legs.

The *gallbladder meridian* at the highest point of the cheekbones brings the life force into the upper digestive organs, the hip joints, and the knees down to the toes.

The *bladder meridian,* which begins at the root of the nose near the eyebrows, brings the life force over the head, down the spinal column to the buttocks, and down the back side of the legs to the small toes. The beginning points are easy to find. They feel as If you were touching a very fine magnet.

Once again, here is an overview that shows how this exercise can contribute to your well-being:

LIGHT-CHANNEL HEALING ON THE FACE HAS A HEALING EFFECT FOR

Physical complaints such as
sleeplessness – dizziness – weak stomach – toothache – flatulence – backache – pain in the knees or ankles, hip pain – headache – sore throat – chest problems – asthma – bladder complaints

Emotional problems such as
agitation – feelings of stress – sorrow – frustration – impatience – fears – helplessness – anger – indecisiveness

Releasing the Back of the Head

The touch of your two hands on the back of the head can contribute much to a harmonious flow of the life energy. If you suffer from a headache and dizziness or just aren't able to calm your thoughts, this exercise can bring you relief. Place your hands flat on the back of the head, with the thumbs on the transition to the neck, for about five minutes. This releases the blockages in the *gallbladder* and *bladder meridian*. The blockages at the back of the head are frequently the cause of sleep disorders. You will be amazed at how wonderfully the Light Channel begins to flow in the entire head, the back, pelvis, hips, knees, and ankles! The head will feel lighter and more space will be created in your soul for inner calmness.

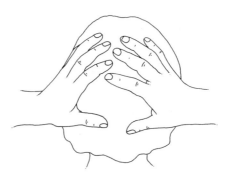

Releasing the back of the head

LIGHT-CHANNEL HEALING AT THE BACK OF THE HEAD HAS A HEALING EFFECT FOR

Physical complaints such as
headache – dizziness – weak sight – neck tension – pain in the hip joints – knee pain – backache – sleep disorders – bladder problems

Emotional problems such as
fears – impatience – nervousness – anger – indecisiveness – helplessness

Light-Channel Healing on the Collarbone

If you suffer from blockages in the neck and throat area, this exercise will be helpful. These blockages in the Light Channels obstruct a harmonious flow through the throat from the head down into the lower areas of the body. They are the cause of sleep disorders, high blood pressure, headache, congestion, pressure on the ears, jaw and tooth problems, dizziness, and much more. When the neck is tense, and the energies no longer flow freely from the arms to the head. This can lead to pain in the shoulder joint and in the arms and fingers.

Place the fingertips of both hands gently on the upper edge of the collarbones. You will find the collarbone as the cross connection to the shoulders on each side beneath the neck. Let your fingers rest at this point for about five minutes.

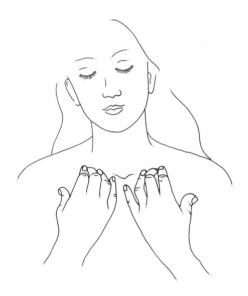

Hands on the collarbone

Since this exercise stimulates the *stomach meridian* in particular, it helps against motion sickness because this type of Light-Channel work releases blockages in the head, jaw, neck, stomach, abdomen, knees, and feet. It allows the energy to flow in a soothing way from the head to the feet.

The belly, abdomen, and legs are once again filled with energy. Even the feet can be warmed through this light touch!

The following overview shows you which emotional and physical complaints can be positively influenced through this gentle touch:

LIGHT-CHANNEL HEALING ON THE COLLARBONE HAS A HEALING EFFECT FOR

Physical complaints such as
travel complaints, sensitive stomach – headache – dizziness – toothache – ear problems – eye inflammations – sore throat – bronchitis – stomach complaints – digestive complaints – cold feet – abdominal complaints – knee pain – skin problems – eczema

Emotional problems such as
stress – fatigue – states of exhaustion – rejection – feelings of repulsion – doubts – being obsessively critical – rigidity

Light-Channel Healing on the Knees

When you use the simple touch of the knees shown below, you will quickly feel that the knees are connected to the head. Light-Channel work also stimulates an entire system of flowing channels in this area: In addition to the *stomach meridian*, this is where you will also find the *gallbladder meridian*, which flows down from the head to the feet. The knee also has a correlation to the head. It could almost be called a small-scale head. As a result, we can also treat complaints such as a headache or toothache on the knees. (Be sure to also clarify the situation with your doctor if the complaints continue!)

Touching the knees like this stimulates the energy flow from the head to the feet! This exercise is also beneficial for those who work at the computer because of the strong blockages that frequently manifest in the jaw, neck, and chest area (as mentioned above).

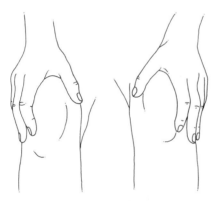

Hands on the knees

Grasp both knees with your hands. Place the thumb on the inner side of the knees, the other fingers on the outer side. Stay quietly in this position for at least five minutes. This will feel good.

You will soon sense how the energy is flowing downward from the head through the belly and the pelvis. The legs and feet will also be flooded with new energy.

LIGHT-CHANNEL HEALING ON THE KNEE HAS A HEALING EFFECT FOR

Physical complaints such as
toothache – ear complaints – feelings of hunger – asthma
– stomach complaints – digestive complaints – headache
– high blood pressure – circulatory complaints – pain in
the knees and feet – hip-joint pain

Emotional problems such as
bitterness – rejection – doubts – anger – rage – feeling
aggravated – desire for revenge

The Tips of the Toes

As in the fingertips, the ends of the toes also contain easily stimulated beginning and ending points for the six channels. Warm yang energy flows from the head to the tips of the toes. If this does not occur, the feet are usually cold because the cooling yin energy receives too little stimulation for it to flow upward. As a result, it congests in the feet and lower legs. The channels of the corresponding organs then receive too little life energy.

In the same way as releasing the fingertips, hold the toes by the nail bed between your thumb and index finger. The following illustration repeats the information on the beginning and ending points of the meridians from Point 13 in the chapter on "Light-Channel Therapy as Healing for Fellow Humans" on page 61.

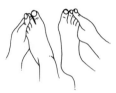

Releasing the tips of the toes

Three yang meridians end at the tips of the toes:
stomach meridian – bladder meridian – gallbladder meridian.

The three yin channels begin here:
spleen meridian – liver meridian – kidney meridian

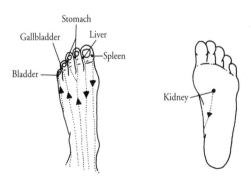

Ting points on the toes and in the middle of the foot

The ting point for the *bladder meridian* is located on the outer side of the nail bed of the little toe. Circle this point between the thumb and the index finger with care and sensitivity. For the second toe, stimulate the ending point of the *gallbladder meridian.* The two next toes (third and fourth) are the ending point of the *stomach meridian.* Both sides of the nail bed on the big toe are the beginning points of the two yin meridians: *spleen* and *liver.* The beginning point of the *kidney meridian* is located at the middle of the sole of the foot on the underside of the foot.

Light-Channel work on the toes has a very relaxing effect on the entire organism. As mentioned above, this stimulates the harmonious balance between the active yang energy and the passive yin energy, as well as the corresponding elements.

> The energy of the *gallbladder meridian* (yang) is transferred from the *liver meridian* (yin) and sent upward to the rib area. These two currents form a pair from the element *wood.*

> The *bladder meridian* (yang) sends its energy to the *kidney meridian* (yin) and together they form a pair from the element *water.*

> The *stomach meridian* (yang) sends its energy to the *spleen meridian* (yin) and together they form a pair from the element *earth.*

LIGHT-CHANNEL HEALING AT THE TIPS OF THE TOES HAS A HEALING EFFECT FOR

> Physical complaints such as
> skin problems – eczema – digestive disorders – varicose veins – hemorrhoids – incontinence – potency disorders – bladder weakness – kidney weakness – headache – dizziness – circulatory complaints

> Emotional problems such as
> fear – fright – frustration – superstition – apprehension – indecisiveness – anger – pride – desire for revenge – rage

Light-Channel Healing on the Sternum

The *conception vessel* at the center of the body brings yin energy upward from below, running from the pubic bone to the lower lip. This main current rules all of the yin meridians. If you touch this Light Channel with your fingertips, you will stimulate all of the yin meridians at the same time. This touch has a calming and cooling effect. The left side of the body is connected to this main vessel.

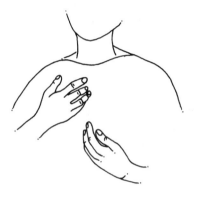

Touching the sternum

At the lips, the energy is passed on to the *directing (governor) vessel* and flows on to the upper lip, over the head, and down the middle of the back to the perineum. Touching this Light current is stimulating and warming since it influences all of the yang meridians.

Light-Channel work on the sternum is wonderfully harmonizing in cases of inner agitation and tension. Use your fingertips to touch all of the points on the middle line of your body between the solar plexus and the neck. This touch is very relaxing and an outstanding sedative. This easy exercise has also proven to be very effective against hot flashes during menopause.

We can use these simple exercises to have invaluable experiences on ourselves and discover: This new form of health care is simple, and we can quickly learn to feel the flow of the meridians. Fortunately, our sensitivity has become so strongly developed in recent years that increasingly more people feel drawn to this new form of therapy—and I am certain that it will appeal to even more groups of people in the future. In this way, the true causes of health disorders can be recognized in due time. Embedded within these perceptions, a trusting knowledge deepens that the energy body is fed from the all-encompassing primordial Divine Light—a Light that awakens love, joy, and kindness within us. Light-Channel work is not only necessary for physical health, it is simultaneously a new orientation toward the higher vibration of the Christ Light. Every health disorder or emotional disharmony should first be treated by Light-Channel work because reinstating a harmoniously flowing energy system is the basis for the physical and emotional healing process.

LIGHT-CHANNEL HEALING ON THE STERNUM HAS A HEALING EFFECT FOR

Physical complaints such as
tension – hot flashes – menopausal complaints – digestive disorders – heart and lung diseases – speech disorders – backache

Emotional problems such as
inner tension, fears – nervousness – impatience

Self-Healing through Meditation

We should not overlook an important possibility for self-healing: meditation or inner silence. Meditation on a regular basis is an outstanding way to heal ourselves. In the stillness, we open ourselves for the all-encompassing Cosmic Light. This strengthens the Light in our aura and activates the flow of the life force.

During meditation, we practice not only the soothing quieting of thoughts, but also recognize and observe our thoughts and feelings. In this stillness, consciousness is opened to the highest dimensions of the Light. Intuition and creativity can gently flow in through this state of peace. In addition, the inner stillness makes it possible for us to subtly perceive the feelings in our chakras. This awareness alone has a healing effect and transforms oppressive feelings. In this stillness, our chakras become free of blockages and the flow of the meridians is filled with renewed strength.

Active thinking distances us from core of our own inner nature—our center. In this process, we are occupied with the past or with the future. However, we must always recognize that thoughts are very *creative* energies because they continuously give rise to our reality! This is why it is extremely important that we think about what we really like and not about what we don't like! With our own thoughts, we continuously weave our earthly destiny. Yet, spiritual development always occurs during the brief moments when the thoughts are quiet. In this process, our self-awareness grows in a very subtle way. Self-awareness helps relieve emotional suffering because it teaches us to observe and control thought patterns

In complete stillness, we feel our inner state that consists of feelings and emotions. However, this feeling of the emotions must initially be developed. Only in the stillness does it become possible, only the quieting of the thoughts allows us to become conscious of our emotional nature! Perceiving our feelings has a transformational healing power that is inconceivable. When we feel the fear, it dissolves! When we feel the mourning and cry the tears, the sorrow dissolves! Feel the envy, the ill will, and much more! When we perceive our deepest, suppressed feelings, we see how they are released into the Light!

Meditation also develops our growth toward the Light in other ways because only the stillness makes the merging of vibrational frequencies from higher dimensions possible. The inner Light begins to shine; even if there occasionally is a veil over the Light—the Light is always there. Just like the sun is hidden by the clouds now and then, these rain clouds still bring growth and fertility to the Earth. A constantly shining sun would be disastrous, and the greatest spiritual growth occurs through crises and suffering.

Meditation increases our vibration and attitude toward the spiritual Light world and the heavenly helpers. A few minutes of meditation every day and entering into the stillness opens up entirely new dimensions of consciousness for us. Our aura and energy system become filled fresh life force, we can subtly perceive blockages and release them. This makes meditation the foundation of our spiritual development, self-realization, and self-healing.

Deeper Knowledge
about
the Laws of the Life Force

The Five Elements—
Grounded in the Light of the Angels

YOU ARE A CHILD OF GOD, YOU ARE
BORN FROM THE LIGHT, LIVE THROUGH
THE LIGHT, AND SHINE IN THIS WORLD.

MESSAGE FROM THE ANGELS

Now that we have become familiar with the practical approach to treatment for clients and for ourselves, this chapter will explain the deeper correlates of Light-Channel Healing. Light-Channel work is a subtle, natural method of treatment that is built on a solid foundation. Basic knowledge about the energy system, the meridians, and the chakras should be a component of general education because they are part of our nature. It is still not possible to measure some of the energies, but we can feel them—and this with increasing accuracy as our sensitivity develops more and more in the near future.

Traditional Chinese Medicine, from which the theory of meridians explained here also originates, has handed down a very good system regarding the powers of the elements. According to this perspective, everything is influenced by the effective powers of the five elements—outside in nature and inside the body. Whatever takes place in nature also occurs in the body in the same way. Paracelsus, the great physician of the Middle Ages, maintained a holistic perspective of the human body functions and left us this beautiful sentence:

"NATURE IS A HUMAN BEING TURNED
INSIDE OUT,
AND THE HUMAN BEING IS NATURE
TURNED INWARD."

According to Traditional Chinese Medicine, there are five different elements that interact with each other. They embody the principles that maintain harmony in the human body, in living spaces (feng shui), in the interplay of nature, and in the cosmos through the spiritual forces of order.

The five elemental forces

GOD CREATED THE MICROCOSM (THE HUMAN BEING)
TO REVEAL ALL OF THE NATURAL MYSTERIES,
SO THAT WHAT IS INVISIBLE WILL BECOME VISIBLE.

PARACELSUS

Interplay of the Elements in Nature and in the Body

In the midst of the natural forces, we live embedded in a grandiose order of Light and power fields. The liveliness and mobility of nature and the body are ruled by the same components and principles. Nature is big, and the body is a scaled-down replica of it. The Five Element Theory is confirmed for us in the attentive observation of nature: On the one hand, the elements support each other, but on the other hand they regulate each other so that no uncontrolled growth takes place.

We can observe how the elements support each other: wood develops out of water, and the wood nourishes the fire. Fire feeds the earth as a fertilizer, and metal is formed within the earth, and this nourishes the water in the form of mineral salts.

We can also observe how the elements control each other: Fire in the earth inhibits the propagation of metal, minerals (metal) control the growth of wood. Through its growth, wood controls the earth, and earth controls water in its expansion. Water inhibits and cools fire.

The following overview provides a clear summary of these elements:

The elements keep each other in balance through support or limitation. In nature—as well as in the body of all living beings—there is a struggle to maintain this balance.

THE NOURISHING CYCLE:

Water	→	Wood
Wood	→	Fire
Fire	→	Earth
Earth	→	Metal
Metal	→	Water

THE CONTROLLING CYCLE:

Fire	→	Metal
Earth	→	Water
Metal	→	Wood
Water	→	Fire
Wood	→	Earth

Many of the processes in nature are reflected in a small-scale form within our own body. Fire (sun) gives the water its power of evaporation. In nature, clouds are formed. In the human body, water primarily evaporates through the lungs. Rain is the water that falls to the earth and brings growth and flourishing. After this metabolization, it seeps into the ground. It unites in the ground water and flows through streams and rivers back to the sea. In the body, food and liquids are ingested and assimilated in the digestive tract. The water is eliminated through the kidneys and collects in the bladder like the ground water in the earth. The life force and developmental powers are maintained in a great variety of ways through the five elements.

We are part of nature. Whatever has become disharmonious in nature has the same effect on the metabolism of humans and all living beings. Consequently, every disharmony in the natural basis of life has an effect on the state of health for all living beings.

It is easy to observe the five transformational phases of the elements during the course of the day. The early morning begins with the rising of the sun. This is when the element of *wood* activates growth and unfolding. At midday, the sun is at its highest point and supports the complete development since the element of *fire* corresponds with full development, with activity and the love of life. Then the sun moves toward the west, and a calming occurs in the later afternoon. This phase corresponds with the element of *earth*. Twilight marks the beginning of the evening. Activity subsides, and the element of *metal* brings a preserving, embracing, and calming effect with it. At midnight, the peace and quiet and darkness have reached their peak. The element of *water* reflects the greatest compression. This is a time of collection and dissolution.

The course of the year also follows the same principles of transformation through the seasons. Even the directions, colors, psychic energies, organs, body fluids—actually, everything that exists—correspond to the principles of the five elements and the invisible forces at work behind them.

The next illustration shows a summary of the various cycles of the five elements—the wide spectrum in the play of the forces of nature and living beings.

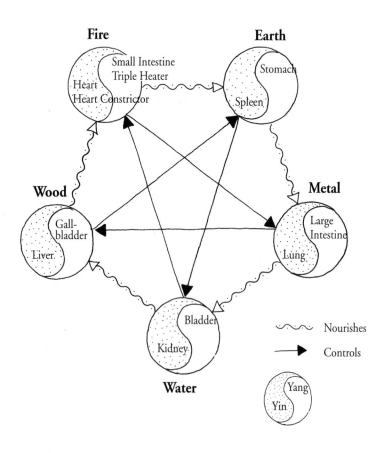

Cycle of the five elements

The Five Elements
in the Spectrum of Correlates

Classification	WOOD	FIRE	EARTH	METAL	WATER
Meridian	**Liver**	**Heart**	**Spleen**	**Lung**	**Kidney**
	Gallbladder	**Small Intestine**	**Stomach**	**Large Intestine**	**Bladder**
		Heart Constrictor			
		Triple Heater			
Direction	East	South	Center	West	North
Season	Spring	Summer	Late Summer	Autumn	Winter
Time of Day	Morning	Midday	Afternoon	Evening	Night
Climate	Wind	Heat	Moisture	Dryness	Cold
Color	Green	Red	Yellow	White	Blue
Body Tissue	Muscles Tendons	Blood Vessels	Connective Tissue Fat	Skin Body hair	Bones Teeth
Joints	Shoulders	Elbows	Hips	Wrists	Knees
Pain	Wandering	Vehement	Dull	Increasing	Constant
Sensory Organs	Eyes	Tongue	Mouth, Lips	Nose	Ears
Sensory Function	Vision	Speech	Taste	Smell, Touch	Hearing
Body Fluids	Tears	Sweat	Saliva, Lymph	Mucous	Urine
Taste	Sour	Bitter	Sweet	Spicy	Salty
Emotional Expression	Screaming	Laughing	Singing	Crying	Sighing
Stress Behavior	Controlling	Clearing the Throat	Burping	Coughing	Trembling
Psychic Energy	Creativity Tolerance Defense	Optimism Respect Contentment	Care Self-Confidence Equilibrium	Vitality Reliability Order	Will Initiative Courage
Destructive Energy	Anger Depression	Dissatisfaction Hysteria	Brooding Worrying	Sadness Grief	Fear Fright
Excessive Energy	Vengeance	Weight Loss	Uneven Temper	Stubbornness	Impulsiveness
Deficient Energy	Complaining	Depression	Laziness	Dissolution	Fright
Sexuality	Passion	Love	Tenderness	Letting Go	Drive
Functions	Production Detoxification	Assimilation Transportation	Nutrient Supply Digestion	Absorption Elimination	Filtration Withdrawal

Archangels as Spiritual Guardians of the Elements

The superficial world of the senses is not the true reality of life. True reality is an indescribable Light world that affects the various vibrational planes, is reflected in its correlates, and only becomes visible to us as the last stage. The spiritual plane is inseparably connected with our consciousness since everything is equally permeated with the power of spirit or Light. The angels make sure that there is a good communication between the source of the Divine Light and its creations in the visible world.

The elements also have their roots as a principle in the spiritual order of Light, but they have an effect as correlates in the Light Channels and organs of the body. Light-Channel Healing harmonizes the elements and views them from both the spiritual and the material plane. All Light Channels are subject to the elements and the forces of the angels. Angels are at work in the tides, the rivers and oceans, the sun, the grass, the snow, and the singing of the birds. Nature and human beings are created according to the same laws and energetic patterns. Subtle matrixes create forms from spirals, crystals, and mandalas. The entire Creation is interwoven with invisible spiritual forces.

Below is my interpretation of how the Chinese elements are associated with the high angelic forces that I see as the guardians of the respective elements and which support our Light-Channel work.

ELEMENT OF FIRE
with the small-intestine and heart meridian,
triple-heater and heart-constrictor meridian
From the divine abundance of Light and power, the Archangel *Michael* with a sword of Light assertively transmits enthusiasm for God's love. He protectively opens the hearts of human beings for the warming sun of Light. The laws of the element of fire are subject to him on both the spiritual and the material plane.

Element of Earth
with the stomach and spleen meridian
With much devotion and love, the Archangel *Uriel* gives us bright Light for the assimilation and transformation of the Earth toward the Light. He brings the truth about the divine world of Light into the consciousness of human beings in a gentle way. The laws of the element of earth are subject to him on all levels.

Element of Metal (Air)
with the large-intestine and lung meridian
Like a delicate breeze, the Archangel *Raphael* lets the healing currents of the light flow into the bodies of all living beings. His Light is the healing, structuring force in reconnecting with the Light order of the higher levels. The laws of the elements of metal (air) are subject to him on all levels.

Element of Water
with the bladder and kidney meridian
Like a strong white Light, the Archangel *Gabriel* is at work in everything and spreads unfolding and flourishing throughout Creation. With the forces of the moon and other structuring factors, his function is the most important transmitter of spiritual information through the movement of water. The element of water is subject to him on all levels.

Element of Wood
with the gallbladder and liver meridian
The power of Archangel *Nathanael* is as dynamic as the awakening of spring. His power accompanies us in the current age of transformation. His light-green radiant Light is very concentrated. His power is present in everything that has a new beginning, that wants to expand and grow. The element of wood is subject to him on all levels.

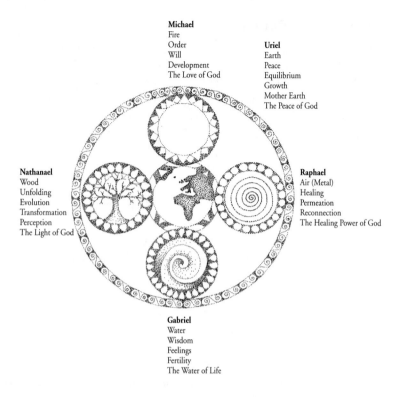

Michael
Fire
Order
Will
Development
The Love of God

Uriel
Earth
Peace
Equilibrium
Growth
Mother Earth
The Peace of God

Nathanael
Wood
Unfolding
Evolution
Transformation
Perception
The Light of God

Raphael
Air (Metal)
Healing
Permeation
Reconnection
The Healing Power of God

Gabriel
Water
Wisdom
Feelings
Fertility
The Water of Life

The five elements and the powers of the archangels

THIS IS WHY WE SHOULD UNDERSTAND ART IN THE SENSE
THAT THERE IS NO OTHER REASON FOR IT THAN THAT WE
SEEK IT WITH THE LIGHT ALONE THAT WE POSSESS IN NATURE
ITSELF AND IN THIS LIGHT IS FOUND WHAT NO ONE KNOWS;
AND WITHOUT THIS LIGHT ALL THINGS REMAIN IN THE
DARKNESS, IN WHICH NOTHING AT ALL CAN BE SOUGHT.

Paracelsus

Meditation:
Connecting with the Protective Power of the Archangels

Michael - Gabriel - Raphael - Uriel - Nathanael

Here is a meditation designed to help us relax and unwind. With its help, we can feel the power of the archangels and the elements in a very subtle way from within. Even just reading it silently has a beneficial effect!

I rest in the center of my being and feel the flow of my breath…

Thoughts come and go, but I am indifferent to them. There is nothing that I want to achieve. I allow it to happen. A deep calmness spreads, and my inner world expands… My feet touch the ground. They are warm and open. I feel the connection to the power of the Earth through my buttocks and through my feet… With the crown chakra above my head, I open myself to the higher dimensions of the universe. The heavenly Light gently flows over me and through me from my head to my feet… With every breath, I am connected with the forces of heaven and Earth. The loving forces breathe through me and envelop me in a harmonious cycle every time I inhale and exhale. A deep sense of security spreads within me…

Everything is silent and rich. In my deep repose, I increasingly feel the connection to Divine Being. I imagine how Light rays are flowing in all directions, as if they were coming from a radiant, spiritual sun. Angelic beings spread this Light as infinite Love, kindness, and compassion throughout all of nature. They work through me and are always there when I call them…

I invoke the protection and the healing power of the mighty archangels: Michael, Gabriel, Raphael, Uriel, and Nathanael…

On my right, masculine, active side stands Michael, the mighty figure of Light. His name means: Who is like God. He appears in the radiance of the sun. My right side is my sunny side. With his radiant sword of Light, he protects the Light of my soul. He helps me to recognize the light and dark aspects within my soul so that I spread the love of the Divine Light upon this Earth… With his sword, he opens the closed portals of my heart and inflames the fire of love within me. As the Prince of the Sun, he rules over the element of fire… In the fire of love, I sense his power. And the love glows very delicately in my heart… The sun is the most beautiful symbol of the Creative Light and its Archangel Michael… My luminous Light body and the heat of my body are subject to his power… In my digestive juices, I feel the element of fire at work… Every flame is an expression of him. And deep in the soil beneath my feet lies a mighty fireball… and this is where his effect is incredibly powerful. All levels of the fire are the emanating Light of God. Archangel Michael rules over them.

To my left, feminine, passive side stands the mighty figure of Light Gabriel with a radiant, loving kindness. His name means: the power of God. As the proclaimer of all life, he is connected with the forces of the moon and fertility… In the mystery of conception and the incarnation of the soul I sense his creative wisdom and power… He preserves pure, spiritual patterns of structure, made visible as the most beautiful crystals, in the element of water… The left side of my body is the feminine, feeling side. He helps me, through feeling and trust, to develop the divine wisdom in my soul… He gives me the water of life as I open myself like an empty vessel and let life happen… Wisdom and intuition flow into my consciousness and make me flexible and open for a happy existence on this Earth… Archangel Gabriel makes me alive and moved through my feelings and tears. My body is soft and flexible through the water … Water is fertility and cleansing on all levels. All the springs, rivers, and oceans are the basis of our life. All levels of the water are the emanating Light of God. The Archangel Gabriel rules over them.

Behind me stands the radiant Archangel Raphael with a raised, protective hand. His name means: God heals. He spreads the breath of God as healing Light into matter… His violet wings of Light flow around me like a delicate protective mantle... He lovingly watches over the harmonious currents of Light throughout the entire Creation. He lovingly brings order to wherever disharmony rules because he spreads divine wisdom through healing Light... The element of metal or air is subject to him. He rules over a harmonious order of Light as peace and stillness... I feel these delicate Light currents in my chakras and meridians as wonderful life energy... Through my loving thoughts and imagination I spread spiritual rays of Light among my fellow human beings... With his support, I spread the healing vibrations of Light to wherever I send them... He stands by me and guides my hands when I transmit healing energy to my fellow humans... I see the clouds in the sky and how they are moved by the winds... I hear the rushing of the waves of water, moved by the wind... I hear the rustling of the leaves in the trees... A delicately gentle breeze penetrates me with breath... Within my digestion is living movement... The love of God flows like a delicate breath of wind through my body... Archangel Raphael rules over it.

The radiant figure of Uriel stands in front of me. His name means: God is Light. As the warming angel of the sun, he watches over the various dimensions of the earth element with his golden Light... His illuminating Light penetrates into the entire Creation and into every cell of my body... He brightens everything that is dark... Time and again he lovingly whispers his encouragement and cheers me up when I believe I am in darkness and doubts darken my mind. With his radiant Light he shows me the way into this life on Earth... I see the blue planet Earth in the cosmos... The Earth is a wonderful living being... Like a great mother, she bears all life in the love play with the penetrating Light... I see high mountains and green hills in the sunlight... In my body there are bones that give me solidity and support... In my soul, courage and steadfastness are my strengths... The Light of God condenses into the element of earth... Archangel Uriel watches over it.

Above me floats a powerful figure of Light. It is the Archangel Nathanael. Like the springtime sun brings the development of new life or every sunrise in the morning produces a new day, the love plan of God desires a renewal of our consciousness. Everything that should be created anew, that grows and thrives, that is planned and carried out, is subject to the element of wood. Archangel Nathanael bestows the renewal and transformation of the Earth and all creatures of the Earth on a higher vibrational plane... We *approach the Light of God and feel increasingly stronger in its presence… Everything is in a state of change… My consciousness has no limits… I can expand into the cosmos… I can expand into a mysterious dimension outside of time and space… All information is anchored in my consciousness… My body is a replica of the entire Earth… I carry all the information of the Earth in my body. My soul is a ray of God's Light. Nothing happens that is not anchored in the wisdom of God's plan. Archangel Nathanael lovingly watches over this.*

A strong energy of love gently and tenderly envelops me… The five powerful figures of Light connect with their wings and form a protective circle of Light around me… As in a delicate protective mantle, I am lovingly enveloped… I feel a sense of security and sense that everything dark and heavy in my life is being released into the Light… It becomes increasingly lighter within me and around me. Joy and bliss grow within me… Deep gratitude fills my heart… Healing Light is now everywhere, in every corner of the room, in the whole city, and it spreads across the entire Earth …

I imagine a fellow human being who is suffering, who needs this wonderful power of Light, and ask the archangels for their healing circle of Light… I see how this person, who I am now thinking of, is lovingly enveloped in a circle of Light. And I see how high spirits and cheerfulness fill my fellow human in the healing glow of the Light…

From the bottom of my heart, I thank the powerful five heavenly messengers and know that they are there for me whenever I call upon them and need their healing Light for myself or for others.

The Living Rhythm of the Organ Clock

BE ALIVE AND FLEXIBLE
IN THE FLOW OF LIFE.
THEN YOU WILL SUFFER LESS!
MESSAGE FROM THE ANGELS

The following section provides in-depth information about the rhythm of the inner organ clock. This knowledge is not absolutely necessary for successful Light-Channel work, but it is very interesting and deepens our awareness of the subtle laws related to life energy.

Everything is subject to the law of rhythm. This is one of the ancient Hermetic principles and has proved itself in view of the inner organ clock. The energy channels with the associated body organs are subject to phases of more or less activity. In the course of the 24 hours of the day, each of the Light Channels with its corresponding organ alternately receives an increased amount of energy over a time period of two hours.

The fluctuating activities of the organs, hormones, and metabolism are created by the steady rhythm of the inner clock. At night, the organs of the liver, gallbladder, and lungs are alternately in their active phase. Complaints are often perceived during these times and provide corresponding information about a possibly disharmonious energy supply to the organs. For example:

 Difficulties in falling asleep between 11 p.m. and 1 a.m. arise during the active phase of the gallbladder meridians.

 Awakening at night between 1 a.m. and 3 a.m. occurs during the active phase of the liver meridians.

 Nightly coughing between 3 a.m. and 5 a.m. occurs during the active phase of the lung meridian.

The organ clock helps us to consciously experience the day and night rhythm of the body. For example:

 In the morning between 5 a.m. and 7 a.m. we experience the active phase of the large-intestine meridians, which normally stimulates the need to relieve the bowels.

 We feel the need for our first meal between 7 a.m. and 9 a.m. during the active phase of the stomach meridian. This is why breakfast should be rich. Nausea in the morning indicates a disorder of the stomach meridian.

The information in the following illustration makes it possible for us to observe our own inner rhythm, as well as that of others. Knowledge about these inner "organ times" is helps us to recognize and eliminate health disorders and disharmonies in the energy system through attentive observation. Done in due time, this can prevent problems from manifesting in the respective organ.

When a meridian is at the climax of its activity, the opposite meridian is in its passive phase. At the time of the greatest organ activity, there is usually an intensification of health disorders such as: pain, heat, feelings of tension, lack of energy, weakness, failure to function, cold, or disorders related to sensations.

The head area and the brain have a resting phase at night. During this time, the energy is mainly active in the inner organs of the gallbladder, liver, and lungs. However, when blockages in the Light Channels at the back of the head, nape of the neck, and neck obstruct the energy flow, too much energy remains in the head area and causes sleep disorders. Through Light-Channel Healing, we can release these blockages at the back of the head–and the long-desired nighttime rest sets in again without the use of medications!

By consulting the organ clock, we can recognize which channels are participating in the disorders and where specific blockages can be released through the Light-Channel treatment so that the inner rhythm stays in harmony with the cosmic orchestra of Light and love. The following illustration also depicts the energy cycle in a clockwise direction.

Meridians and organ clock

An Example from My Practice

A 40-year-old man sought my help in healing his complaints: He had been suffering from a major sleep disorder for quite a while. It took him a long time to fall asleep and he would lay awake for hours every night. As a result of the sleep deficit, he felt very exhausted and nervous. He had, of course, tried all of the medical possibilities—but not even sleeping tablets could help him.

1st Treatment

I discovered a very strong blockage at the back of the head. The shoulders had an abundance of warm yang energy. But the body felt cold from the belly down. My client had previously had an operation on the left knee, and had presumably been experiencing a disharmony in the Light

Channels for a long time. There was too much energy in the upper area and too little from the pelvis downward. I did a Light-Channel treatment from his head to his feet. I focused particularly on releasing the back of the head.

2nd Treatment (4 weeks later)

My client returned with a great deal of enthusiasm. He had slept better than he had in a long time. He sometimes even went to bed at 9 p.m. and slept through the entire night! His shoulders were still blocked and painful. Blockages in the back were also released during his complete Light-Channel treatment.

3rd Treatment (3 months later)

His physical and emotional condition was now very good once again. He pointed out that even his co-workers noticed the major change that had taken place within him. I give him one more complete treatment.

Since then, this man returns about once a year to be re-harmonized by the Light-Channel therapy. During his most recent visit, he was very blocked and the left side of his body—including the shoulders and chest—reacted with pain. The cause was late night hours working at the computer. Unfortunately, the radiation from these devices can have a very negative influence on the energy system! After sitting at the computer for a longer period of time, it is helpful to balance and ground the energy system by taking a walk through nature. Otherwise, the client's sleeping disorders had been wonderfully eliminated through the treatment.

Spiritual Development
and
Psychic Abilities

The Home of Our Soul

DIVINE LIGHT IS FOLDED
INTO YOUR HEART
LIKE A SPARKLING DIAMOND.
TRUST IN YOURSELF
FROM YOUR INNERMOST BEING.
MESSAGE FROM THE ANGELS

Light-Channel Healing means reunification with the Light of heaven. My experiences have shown me that an indescribably powerful source of Light rules over and through us. This Light is radiantly white and has a beautiful geometric organizing structure. It behaves like a huge firework display. I interpret what I have seen in visions as creative primordial Light. It creates all living beings and unceasingly flows into the visible earthly realm as the renewing force from the invisible spiritual background. I consider this Light that is in everything—in human beings to the same degree as in the entire cosmos—to be the effective power of God and call it the Christ Light. Light-Channel work means opening and integrating toward the Christ Light, which flows like a breath of delicate Light currents through our energy channels.

When we are embedded in the natural forces of the elements, enlivened by a flowing energy system that distributes life force into every cell of the body, we enjoy a more or less harmonious life. The information of the sensory organs binds us to this earthly, transitory world. The individual consciousness is directed at the earthly dimensions. It analyzes, deliberates, takes things apart, and then organizes them.

With an increasingly spiritual state of development, growing out of meditative reflection and inner stillness, the knowledge soon awakens within us that a mysterious Light world works through everything with unspeakable wisdom. This mystery underlying everything is the decisive, immortal dimension. It is the true home of our soul. After all, we have a multi-dimensional nature, rooted with the Earth through the body and touching spiritual dimensions with the mind, which is not bound to either time or space. This level of cosmic consciousness encompasses all of the information about the future and the past, about wishes and hopes—there is nothing in life that is not contained here! This plane is also called the "Akashic Records."

So how can information from the cosmic consciousness be received? By training our abilities of extrasensory perception. Meditation is the basis for this development. Only in the stillness free of any intentions can these delicate currents of information flow into our consciousness. Such information can be perceived as images, words, symbols, or sensations of Light. Instead of our own thinking, it is the brief moments of *non-thinking* that allow us to have such connection with all-encompassing wisdom.

The gift of receiving this subtle information from the cosmic consciousness is called *psychic ability.*

My personal experiences have taught me that we all are accompanied by one or more Light beings. The connection with this loving spiritual guidance allows us to receive subtle spiritual information with which we can give Light-Channel treatments on an even finer level. Here is an explanation of the three most important forms of spiritual perception:

Clairvoyance – Clairaudience – Clairsentience

CLAIRVOYANCE
When the third eye at the center of the forehead opens, the spiritual world of Light becomes visible as colorful Light, images, and visions. This "spiritual seeing" does not take place with the physical eye. These are spiritual perceptions that come through the center of the forehead—usually with closed eyes. We call this "seeing" *clairvoyance.*

CLAIRAUDIENCE
The spiritual guidance can arise in the stillness through words or an inner dialog. When our emotional development unfolds in love and compassion, such inspirations will never be destructive. Instead, they are extremely helpful and beneficial for our well-being and the good of the entire surrounding world. The throat chakra becomes a portal for the "holy language" of the cosmic consciousness for this type of spiritual listening. We call this silent listening within and receiving the subtle vibrations of words or sounds *clairaudience.*

CLAIRSENTIENCE

The refinement of our ability to perceive what other people are feeling can become so heightened that it is as if we actually were the other person. The art of sensitivity is called *empathy* or *clairsentience*, which will be explained in more detail later. This spiritual perception is also not bound to time or space. Independent of whether a person is close to us or far away, we can still learn to feel his or her condition—the mind is absolutely free and knows no limitations of time and space!

SPIRITUAL DEVELOPMENT AND PERCEPTION

In the course of our spiritual development, we learn to increasingly differentiate between the perceptions of the physical sensory organs on the one hand and the spiritual information beyond our own thought processes on the other hand. Spiritual perception is subject to the Higher Self or divine wisdom. However, sensory perception binds our consciousness to the superficial level. The earthly world is a grandiose realm of magic that we help design through our free will and the creative power of thoughts. The spiritual and the earthly flow into each other. However, the Higher Self directs everything in the earthly and supernatural life with the greatest wisdom and intelligence. In harmony with the Christ Light, all dimensions of existence are organized according to the cosmic laws.

Our true nature consists of Light and spirit—trapped in an earthly body. In the invisible world, our thoughts produce creative energy fields that continuously transform into matter. As mentioned above, it is incredibly important to control our thoughts and only think what we truly desire to manifest—instead of what we do *not* want. We are integrated into the creative power of the Light through consciousness and make a major contribution to our own life in this way. Imagination that is charged with emotions—which may be positive or negative—is very likely to turn into reality. The creative force absorbs everything and acts according to its spiritual laws.

We must never forget that love is the strongest force in the universe! Everything that is thought and felt in love connects us with our heavenly helpers—the Light-filled, supportive, flowing forces. Everything that is directed against love causes suffering and pain and blocks the life currents. Heaven is not somewhere outside of us. It has a continuous effect on our life. Light beings stand by us and support this heartfelt connection. Everything flows from the one source into all of the spheres and dimensions. The more strongly our innermost nature is permeated by this Light and life force, the more harmoniously the outer manifestations and circumstances correspond with our own wishes. From the spiritual background, the invisible threads are woven to create everything that we are intended to experience and learn. So let us learn to be in deep agreement with everything that is! This attitude brightens our emotional state.

At the time of death, the transitory, physical body is separated from the true immortal nature, which I call the *soul*. The earthly world serves the soul as a learning matrix for its development toward the Light. Everything in life is moved energy and must express itself through different vibrations in keeping with the spiritual laws. But the soul is immortal and part of the Divine Light. In this life, it connects with the earthly body through the chakras and the flowing energy system. The soul forms a wonderful unity with the body in this way. Light-Channel work offers a helpful possibility for continually maintaining the permeation of the physical body with cosmic Light. The Light currents that flow in the meridians are endowed with a super-intelligent life energy that virtually radiates throughout the body and heals it.

Light-Channel work shows us that unpleasant moods and health disorders frequently have the same cause. If our interest is only directed at the outside—the world of matter—we lose the clarity of the mind. However, the soul becomes as clear as a crystal when our attention is directed at the innermost core of life in stillness and concentration. Then the Light of the spiritual world will be reflected in an increasingly better way. From this stillness, all of the spiritual gifts and even psychic abilities can develop—for each of us. It is important to remember that the spiritual helpers can do their work better when we have learned to remain completely free of thoughts for brief moments. Meditation develops our inner Light, and we become a blessing for our fellow human beings, wherever they may be. Inner stillness gives us peace and harmony, and the outer life also becomes structured in accordance with it.

Psychic Abilities–
State of Consciousness for the
New Age

We are in the middle of a worldwide transformation. Our consciousness is opening to higher vibrations and apparently wants to release itself from the earth-bound dimensions. At the same time, we should not overlook the fact that various forces are now at work, promoting the good on the one hand and harming nature on the other hand. However, when people work against the laws of the spiritual light order, there will inevitably be corrections. Wherever the life force and serenity are weakened, disease (dis-ease) in the body and/or soul will call for corrections. With Light-Channel Therapy, we now have the beneficial possibility for supporting both others and ourselves in such difficult phases of transformation or corrections with loving devotion.

In my seminars, I have repeatedly discovered with joyful astonishment how many of the participants are medially gifted and have already had the corresponding experiences. The development of these spiritual talents is now being intensely accelerated. Sometimes inexplicable perceptions even cause fear because they cannot be classified according to the traditional state of knowledge. However, expanded states of consciousness and psychic abilities will change our lives in the future. It is important to know and experience more about them. Children are already coming into the world with psychic abilities, and we will be able to learn a great deal from them!

We are now living in a world that is globally linked by means of technical devices. At the same time, we are beginning to sense that we are also connected in spirit by being globally linked with everything that is. Cosmic intelligence is the basis of everything expressed on the material plane. We must examine for ourselves whether or not the material manifestations have a positive or destructive effect on our emotional state. Through the above-mentioned global grid of the Christ Light, it will soon perhaps be possible for us to communicate through spirit without technical devices! The opening to the high vibration of the Christ Light occurs through the crown chakra. The expansion to all-encompassing consciousness will give all of us the possibility of extrasensory perception.

In the awareness of this all-encompassing connection, we will also be able to send healing energy over great distances since time and space will not be an obstacle. The healing angels are willing to fulfill our wish and actually bring light and power wherever we direct it with our thoughts. This can also be Light-Channel work! We should also think lovingly of the people who cause us difficulties! A healing ray of light dissolves the difficulties and frees us of vindictive feelings or grudges. Angels of peace fill us with the serenity we desire. Energies are exchanged wherever human beings come together—whether in a restaurant, in a train, or on the street. Wherever we encounter people who are suffering, we can transmit healing energies to them very quietly and with loving eyes and hearts. The energy body of the respective person will absorb this energy. Wherever the love of the heart flows, a healing, invisible ray of light serves as the tender connection in the desired direction.

In summary: Developing psychic abilities means "becoming a vessel" in silence for the reception of spiritual information. In an intimate connection with the divine wisdom, this flows into the consciousness in an intuitive way. A growing refinement of the ability to perceive makes it possible for us to receive insights from an unlimited dimension that extends far beyond our own knowledge. Such spiritual information is only possible when the individual self becomes very small and completely makes space for the higher self through inner stillness. Then a genuine selflessness develops. Genuine selflessness is a spiritual state in which there is no separation in terms of time and space. Stillness is the foundation of this state in which we express love for ourselves, for every human being, and for the entire Creation.

Self-Awareness—Foundation of Spiritual Development

It is not possible for anyone in this earthly life to recognize the Absolute. When we consciously look at and contemplate Creation, we can only be in awe about the enormous wisdom that is at work behind everything—so grandiose that even the content of our own soul is continuously made evident to us. Like magic, we often directly encounter our thoughts and feelings as a material manifestation in the outside world. It sometimes seems as if a daylight projector is displaying the content of our own soul on the screen of everyday life! Encounters, experiences, the behavior of our fellow humans, and even natural phenomena speak to us in a very subtle form of communication. Everyday life becomes very exciting if we become an observer and say: "Yes—I'm carefully watching my 'motion picture'!" We often see our own inadequacies lived out in a drastic way by others and shown to us under the direction of the great wisdom that works through everything. Our everyday life is a grandiose play! Of course, this mirror is sometimes not so easy to bear. However, it is certain that everything we find annoying in our fellow human being, whatever we criticize and would like to change, is our own imperfection. When we are criticized by others and become annoyed, both people are affected. If someone criticizes us and would like us to be different, but we can react in a calm way, then all that remains is the projection of the person who is criticizing. The same principle also applies in the positive sense: What we find wonderful and good in others is actually the beauty of our own soul!

Everyday life is the best textbook. Time and again, we are made aware of situations in order to develop or strengthen our spiritual qualities. Nothing occurs as punishment. Everything happens so we can recognize ourselves in it or complete certain steps of spiritual development. Often processes of suffering are the best preconditions for the development of the soul's light. We should never forget that the spiritual Light world is filled with absolute love. Let us learn to simply *be in agreement*! Love is light, and the living Creation is oriented upon the principle of love.

Our own love opens toward the Light. Love desires unity—not conflict. This helps us recognize which spiritual virtues we can further develop! Our Light body then shines with increasing brightness and is in harmony with the higher, spiritual Light worlds. The more the strength of our aura shines, the more healing power flows from our hands for the beneficial Light-Channel work!

Helpers from the Spiritual World

TRUST! I WILL GIVE YOU A SIGN
SO THAT YOUR TRUST WILL BE STRENGTHENED.

MESSAGE FROM THE ANGELS

Through Light-Channel work, we increasingly become better at recognizing that the power of the spirit knows no limits. All people are our brothers and sisters. Together we live in the immense radiant cosmic body of the Christ Light, which connects everything.

It is good to know that during the Light-Channel work we are always connected with spiritual helpers. On our own, we would hardly be capable of giving someone else true healing. Calling the names of the angels, saints, or high spiritual beings immediately connects us with their Light, which can be perceived by the third eye as streaming Light. I have personally discovered that the name of *Jesus Christ* (in my sincere appeals during a Light-Channel session or otherwise) connects me with the highest intensity of cosmic radiance. However, I would like to emphasize that people with a different background and religious affiliation can obviously call on their own saints and then be given the corresponding radiant power. The cosmos does not recognize any dogmatic ideas and organizations! The cosmos is absolute love, and it wants to generously give this love to us human beings as streaming Light.

Every soul has the disposition for perfection, yet we usually still have much that remains to be developed. The Jewish master and God-man Jesus embodies the highest perfection. Even today, his power is here for us as an immense radiant body of white Light in the spiritual world. Jesus and his followers healed the sick. It appears to me that the true mission of the churches is to heal, and I wish that they would once again become places where people are healed. Priests should also become familiar with Light-Channel work because it would give them the possibility to heal the souls of the people entrusted to them and fill them with the Divine Light. Experiences with Light-Channel work have clearly shown that the soul is healed at the same time as the body when blockages are released.

This is because every blockage in the energy system forms an obstacle for the Light flowing through the body *and* soul.

Calling the holy names makes it possible for us, as mentioned above, to establish contact with the radiant power of the Light being to whom we have appealed. Angels, archangels, Mother Mary, or any of the deities with whom we are familiar are there for us and wait for us to call their name. We can immediately feel how a soothing wave of Light enters our aura. The more we cultivate these contacts, the more the radiant intensity of our healing hands increases.

The Art of Empathy

The following is a description of a possible form of clairsentience that I experience every day. Thanks to this clairsentience, I have been able to develop these new gentle methods of treatment! But even if this ability is undeveloped, it is still possible to do wonderful Light-Channel Healing without clairsentience. Love is the most important power for bringing about healing and being permeated with Light.

Every time we think of a fellow human being, no matter how far away this person may be, a tender connection is established between the two Light bodies. Even just speaking the first and last name in our thoughts is enough to synchronize the vibrations. In this loving way, we can bring about wonderful healing even from a distance.

During the Light-Channel treatment, an empathetic state is already generated during the attunement. The individual self moves into the background, and a union takes place between our Light body and that of the client. In this state of consciousness, our body serves as a seismograph. Through empathy, we feel within our own body the other person's energy circulation, emotions, the flow of the meridians, and where blockages have caused hardened knots within them. We can increasingly perceive the feelings in the other person's chakras as if we were this individual. With attentive feelings, we observe the client's inner condition within ourselves and begin—without the power of our own will—to release these blockages by just sensing them. As I have mentioned before, time and space are not relevant in this state of consciousness. The energy system is flooded anew with the life force. This restores the basis for health and well-being. After this flooding with energy, the physical body usually needs time to complete the healing. This may require up to two weeks.

Empathy, or the gift of feeling with someone, makes it possible to perceive the blockages, pain, and emotions of a fellow human being as if these were our own. As mentioned in a previous chapter, traumas from the past are usually noticed as blocked energy of the neck area in the form of painful feelings or emotions. But the feelings themselves are in the chakras, which form an inseparable unity with the Light Channels.

So how can we recognize emotional pain if it is completely suppressed and concealed in the subconscious mind? What state of consciousness makes it possible for us to attune ourselves with clairsentience to the condition of another human being and perceive this condition? How can we achieve this state?

For Light-Channel Healing, empathy is very helpful because it makes it possible for us to do an individually focused treatment. With the specific practices that I teach in my seminars, it is possible for anyone to easily recognize and promote this gift that slumbers within each of us. Which state helps promote our empathy?

Meditating on a regular basis is the primary precondition and, as already described, it is the foundation of every type of spiritual development. Calming the thoughts activates the right hemisphere of the brain and promotes our extrasensory perception—sympathy and devotion are good preconditions for achieving the alignment between the vibration of the practitioner's Light body and that of the client. This merging is an inner experience—a mutual permeation. The differences between "me" and "you" disappear because the all-encompassing power of Light, which is not bound to the physical realm, knows no limitations of the self. Love and compassion resonate in harmony with the higher consciousness, which now assumes the guidance.

On the other hand, empathy is obstructed by every sense of superiority, artificiality, coldness, willfulness, and setting of boundaries. These qualities create separation and prevent a merging. Only love knows no boundaries and opens us to the Light. Seeing our fellow human beings in the Light, considering them to be brothers or sisters and a divine expression of life, is especially helpful for merging opposites in our Light-Channel work.

The lack of intention found in the meditative, inner stillness strengthens our opening to the spiritual intelligence of the Cosmic Light. This leads us beyond the individual self to unlimited knowledge. Compassionate observation makes us receptive to information that is normally not accessible to the daytime consciousness. In this state of empathy, the emotional or energetic sensations can rise very quietly to the surface and be perceived in a clairvoyant or clairsentient way.

The following perceptions may arise:

- inner images that represent an actual situation in the life of the client

- symbols that depict the emotional situations like a dream image

- colors that show the various vibrations

- inner hearing of insights

- perceiving feelings or sensations within our own body

The foundation of such information is the fact that all circumstances of life are stored in the Light body of each human being. Nothing is lost. Our consciousness is capable of expanding and resonating in these dimensions, which can lead to the beautiful success of our Light-Channel work in the service of our fellow human beings. However, even without the development of these empathetic gifts, our actions for the benefit of others can have their helpful effects!

Cosmic Light on Five Vibrational Planes

In connection with the heavenly helpers, Light-Channel Healing is a blessing for us and our fellow human beings. Our crown chakra forms a wonderful portal for the flowing Light and life force, and opening this chakra makes it possible for us to become a channel or mediator for the flowing Light energy. Healing Light flows out of our fingertips, hand chakras, and hearts into the Light body of those we treat, stimulating the energy currents in their meridians and chakras.

Let's take a closer look at the higher dimensions of Light: The Light order is manifested in pure, geometric forms of energy. Harmony with this cosmic order of Light gives us and our surrounding world true peace that is reflected in the harmony with the cosmic order of Light and its manifestations. All levels of the Creation rest in this immeasurable order of Light: the cosmos, Earth, and human beings. Everything has its correlates, just the vibrational frequencies differ. These vibrational planes are manifested in our body as:

> the spiritual body
>
> the mental body
>
> the emotional body
>
> the etheric body
>
> the physical body

Our spiritual development takes place on each of these levels: from the material world of the senses to the most subtle plane of the Light. Like a tree is rooted in the soil and moves toward the sunlight, the body is bound to the Earth and is flooded with the Cosmic Light.

THE SPIRITUAL BODY

The precondition for empathy during Light-Channel Healing is a developed *spiritual body* with open chakras. Cosmic Light flows in through the crown chakra with a high vibrational frequency that corresponds with that of the spiritual body. Flowing down through all five of the levels, the Light is then transmitted through the chakras to the plane of the physical body. The illusionary separation between us and the great world soul only exists on the vibrational plane of the sensory organs. Healing energy flows from the Cosmic Light, which dwells above us like a radiant sun and exudes love to everything.

THE MENTAL BODY

The vibrational frequency of the mental plane stores the energy fields that we create with our own thoughts. The telepathic transmission of thoughts shows that this plane has no spatial limitations.

At this point, I would like to add something that I experienced while writing this page: I received a call from the client who I mentioned as the first case example in this book. Many months had passed since we last saw each other. She said to me on the telephone that she had repeatedly thought of me lately, and I was able to tell her *why* our thoughts had touched: I had also been mentally in connection with her! Many people have these types of telepathic experiences time and again.

Every thought creates an energy field, which builds up the corresponding resonances in the aura. These resonances directly attract what has been created by the thoughts. New life situations are continuously generated through our mental energies because thoughts and ideas are creative forces. Once again, I would like to emphasize that we must be very careful in dealing with these creative forces: It is extremely important to think of what we really want! If we continuously imagine a situation that we do *not* want, then we practically call it into existence. The universe is the purest love and does not recognize a "no." If we think of what we would like to have in positive expectation and gratitude, our heavenly helpers will send it to us!

The mental level would like to preserve what already exists. It binds the consciousness to the earthly world. This is why it continuously attempts to doubt the delicate intuitive insights. Yet, with the power of higher consciousness we can observe these processes in all stillness and develop increasingly more trust. This helps us overcome the initial doubts about our extrasensory perceptions.

The Emotional Body

The Light energy that permeates everything develops the emotional body through a certain vibrational frequency—a dualistic plane with light and dark aspects. Thinking generates feelings, which may be either cheerful or gloomy, depending on how we evaluate our own life situation. However, with understanding, compassion, and flexibility we become less susceptible to negative feelings—love organizes everything for the good in this respect as well.

The center of our emotional life is the solar-plexus chakra. The lower chakras react strongly to emotional stresses—they can even reverse the direction in which they turn and are then no longer integrated into the Cosmic Light. They shut down when the principles of the cosmic order of love are violated and cause a lack of life energy throughout the entire energy system. Light-Channel work is a wonderful way for us to heal such emotional injuries and problems.

The Etheric Body

A somewhat lower vibrational frequency of the Cosmic Light forms the etheric plane, which models the physical body like a spiritual double and provides the body with life force. In Light-Channel therapy we experience how the twelve meridians and the two main vessels flow on this plane. In addition to these main currents, there are thousands of the finest *nadis,* a very subtle "electrical" network that fills the body and its organs with Light. An intensive intertwining of energy and matter or spirit and body takes place on this plane.

The Physical Body

The five sensory organs—eyes, ears, nose, mouth, and skin—serve the perception of the earthly vibrational frequency. Everything earthly belongs to this plane. This earthly sphere is a narrow spectrum of one breadth of the indescribable dimensions of Light. It is the manifestation of a grandiose order, the matrixes of which form the earthly realm from Light energy. Light gives us strength, life energy, feelings, and thoughts. Light makes the body alive and strong. Light can be manifested as either matter or an invisible force. These are just different vibrational frequencies. So let's enjoy all levels of existence!

Here is a summary of the five most important levels of vibrational frequencies:

SPIRITUAL BODY—COSMIC WISDOM

- Pure consciousness
- No difference between the subject and the object
- Merging of all five levels
- Boundless BEING
- Empathetic connecting
- Opening to the Christ Light

MENTAL BODY—THOUGHT LEVEL

Flowing stream of thoughts with various origins:

- Ego-bound ideas
- Analytical considerations
- Inspirations from the invisible, spiritual plane
- Thought exchange between living beings

EMOTIONAL BODY—LEVEL OF FEELINGS

- Processing and integration of perceptions
- Intellect and thoughts feed this plane
- Dualistic plane of Light and shadow

ETHERIC BODY—LEVEL OF THE LIFE FORCE

- Supplying the body with the life force
- Flowing Light Channels (energy channels)
- Nadis–network of the smallest distribution channels
- Interweaving of energy and matter

Physical Body—Sensory Level

- Hormonal and metabolic activity
- Organ and cell functions
- Power of the five elements

Cosmic Consciousness and Spiritual Development

On the surface, we are caught in an intellectual illusory understanding, yet we can leave this prison and discover an unimaginable freedom. Through meditation, we can let "what is at work behind the appearances" flow more clearly into our consciousness. The material world forms our foundation; its manifestations can be explored and recognized like a mirror of our own consciousness. Spiritual awakening gives us insights, and we can increasingly succeed at connecting the material, superficial level with the spiritual, hidden level. Directly experienced moments of existence are true sources of strength and joy! Intuitive understanding and an absolute lack of intentions give us harmony in everyday life. The possibility of merging with the all-encompassing, inherent Light is constantly there. As we know, spiritual development always takes place in the stillness.

The power of the spirit is eternal and immortal, but the body is earthly and transitory. Now we can promote a harmonious interplay of both levels through the beneficial Light-Channel Healing. Even if this may sound very "grandiose": This work can help us harmoniously unite heaven and earth within the body of the client, activate the creative forces of yin and yang, and increase and stimulate the life force in the process.

Here is a brief summary of what I believe to be the important steps of spiritual development. However, this overview is not intended to convey any type of rigid ideas but encourage others to have their own experiences. Our own experiences give us certainty and trust! And when we let things happen, a great deal can be accomplished!

Spiritual development leads through the following steps:

- Daily meditation opens our consciousness for cosmic wisdom and gives us a sense of detachment from the objects and concerns of the outer world.

- The insight that binding ourselves to the outer world blinds us and creates many types of suffering and worries

- Reviewing the outer circumstances through meditation and contemplation

- Observing our thoughts and feeling our emotions

- Letting go of everything that is directed against the principle of love

- Considering everyday life to be a mirror of the soul in order to recognize ourselves in it

- Experiencing increasingly more Light and unity in the stillness of meditation

- The third eye opening to the spiritual Light world

- Remaining in the contemplation of the Light in all stillness and without intentions

- Letting our own will recede increasingly into the background and surrendering to the higher will

- Now the Heavenly Light can break through and shine

- This Light can appear like a luminous, radiant white sun

- Stillness may be dark—but the Light comes out of the dark

- Becoming one with all things: with the outer manifestation of the Light and the Light within
  This last step releases great forces of the spirit and the Light.

THE HEAVENLY LIGHT APPEARS WHEN A HUMAN BEING
MAINTAINS A STATE OF TOTAL STILLNESS.
WHOEVER RADIATES THE HEAVENLY LIGHT
WILL SEE HIS TRUE SELF.
BY CULTIVATING THE TRUE SELF,
WE ACHIEVE THE ABSOLUTE.
IF SOMEONE ACHIEVES THE ABSOLUTE,
THEN THE HEAVENLY FORCES
WILL RULE OVER HIS EARTHLY LIFE.

CHUANG TZU

Meditation

The following meditation completes this book.

I wish all of my dear readers much Light and joy while doing this wonderful Light-Channel work. May this gentle therapy give many people spiritual and physical well-being!

My eyes show me the solidified form of the Divine Light everywhere I look. I observe everything around me with loving eyes. I perceive all objects in a calm and attentive way. In everything that I see shines the translucent power of Light. I feel this loving power with my heart…

My eyes calmly rest on a tree, a plant, or a fellow human being for a long time. As I do this, my eyes follow the visible contour in a relaxed way and I feel how my heart chakra and forehead chakra expand… My sight becomes a seeing with feeling… My eyes are no longer directed clearly at the object but look unfocused at the background… The inner, spiritual Light shows itself to me very delicately as an aura or ray of Light. I let this happen and become familiar with my clairvoyance in this way.

With the power of my mind, I visualize these soul images in a calm and relaxed way: I find myself on a high mountain. Deep silence and peace reign here. At my feet I see a beautiful, colorful meadow. I look at the colors of the bright flowers… Everything around me pulsates with life and color… Now I see how a wonderful rainbow arches above me. All seven colors of the rainbows flow through my body… I bathe in the seven delicate colors of the rainbow: red – orange – yellow – green – light blue – indigo blue – violet… and feel these beautiful colors… I become one with the colorful Light…

The sun now shines bright and warm, and I experience deep stillness and peace in the warming rays of the sun… I look at the rays and in my state of spiritual contemplation I see Light beings of living, pulsating Light in my state of spiritual observation. I feel how the Light flows into my solar-plexus chakra and is distributed throughout my entire body… I feel a golden Light in my heart chakra—a delicate Light of love... It continually expands and merges with the source of the Light... I feel how the Light expands more and more until I completely merge with the Light. Light beings surround me and lovingly send delicate waves of Light through me. I feel a deep sense of bliss... Healing Light flows through every cell of my body. It organizes and renews everything. More and more, I feel that I am made of Light.

Now I allow myself enough time to look at this wonderful play with my heart

...

The images of my soul now fade slowly. Enriched by this inner experience, I return to my everyday life and feel strengthened and refreshed.

Meridians–
Overview of the Light Channels

The Effects of
Flowing Light and
Blocked Light

Lung Meridian

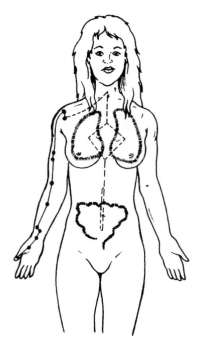

The lung meridian originates in the central abdominal cavity and touches the large intestine there. Both the large-intestine meridian and the lung meridian are associated with the element of air (metal). The Light current of the lung leads upward to the diaphragm, goes into the lungs, and gives them the necessary life force. Under the collarbone, it rises to the surface and can be stimulated with the hands. It flows on the inner side of the upper arms to the elbow, to the lower arm, and ends on the outer side in the tip of the thumb. Another branch forks off over the wrist and goes into the index finger. Here it meets the large-intestine meridian.

▶▶ **Flowing Light:** Humbleness, modesty, cheerfulness, contentment, tolerance

▶▶◀ **Blocked Light:**

PHYSICAL COMPLAINTS:

Health disorders of the respiratory organs, coughing, cold, asthma, shortness of breath, pain in the arms, headache, health disorders in mouth and throat

EMOTIONAL COMPLAINTS:

Depression, contempt, pride, sarcasm, irony, ridicule, remorse

Large-Intestine Meridian

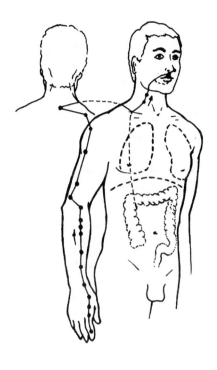

The large-intestine meridian begins at the nail bed of the index finger, flows on the outer side of the index finger to the wrist, continues along the outer side of the lower arm to the outer side of the elbows, then travels on to the upper arm and the highest point on the shoulder. One branch forks off into the inside of the body and flows into the lungs and back down to the large intestine. The other branch remains on the upper side and flows to the neck, across the cheek, and to the inside through the teeth. It ends, after crossing the upper lip, at the nostrils.

▶▶ **Flowing Light:** Enthusiasm, ability to forgive, letting go, generosity

▶▶ **Blocked Light:**

PHYSICAL COMPLAINTS:
> Inflammations in the jaw and neck, colds, congestion, constipation or diarrhea, inflammation of the bowels, high blood pressure, trigeminal neuralgia, toothache

EMOTIONAL COMPLAINTS:
> Worries, feelings of guilt, depression, apathy, indifference, stinginess

Stomach Meridian

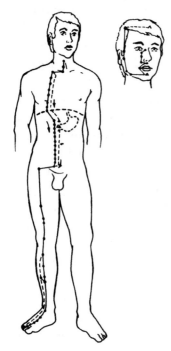

The stomach meridian assumes the energy of the large-intestine meridian at the nostrils, rises inwardly to the root of the nose and comes to the surface beneath the eyes. At the side of the nose, it runs down to the lower jawbones and turns upward in front of the ear at the temples to the cranium, flows back down through the jaw joint to the neck, over the collarbone through the chest, inwardly providing the stomach with life force. Then it flows into the belly down to the groin. From there it flows to the thighs, to the outer side of the knees and over the front center of the lower legs to the tip of the foot. Then it ends at the outer side of the second and third toes. A short branch goes from the instep of the foot to the inner side of the big toe and connects with the spleen channel.

▸▸ **Flowing Light:** Trust, empathy, contentment, adaptability, compassion

▸▸▎ **Blocked Light:**

PHYSICAL COMPLAINTS:

Stomach or intestinal complaints, allergies, migraine, eye diseases, sore throat or toothache, health disorders of the mammary glands, joint pain, skin problems, tension in the jaw area, pain in knees and legs

EMOTIONAL COMPLAINTS:

Rejection, feelings of disgust, bitterness, doubts, excessive criticism of others, disappointment, rigidity

---

Spleen Meridian

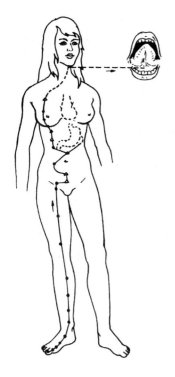

The spleen meridian flows from the outer side of the big toe along the inner side of the foot, in front of the malleoli over the back side of the lower leg and upward to the inner side of the knees and thighs. Here it enters the abdominal cavity. In the inside of the body, the life force from it flows into the spleen, on to the chest, and along the inside to the throat and into the root of the tongue. An inner branch leads into the heart, where it connects with the subsequent heart meridian.

▸▸ **Flowing Light:** Appreciation, confidence, sympathy, trust

▸▸| **Blocked Light:**

PHYSICAL COMPLAINTS:

Stomachache, inflammation of the bowels, flatulence, eczema, and allergies, disorders of the water or blood household, menopausal complaints, vein health disorders, hemorrhoids, bedwetting

EMOTIONAL COMPLAINTS:

Rejection, fear of the future, envy, grimness

Heart Meridian

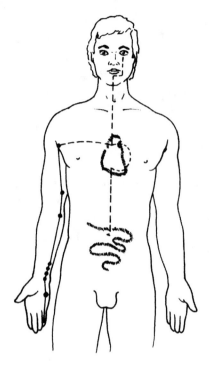

The heart channel originates in the heart. On the inside, a branch runs through the diaphragm into the small intestine and another goes up past the throat to the eye. A third branch runs across the chest, from the heart to the lungs. Then it can be felt on the surface near the armpit. It flows over the inside of the elbow and lower arm to the inside surface of the hand and ends at the nail bed of the small finger on the inner side. There it connects with the small-intestine meridian.

▶▶ **Flowing Light:** Self-confidence, forgiveness, the ability to love, warmth, compassion

▶▶▎ **Blocked Light:**

PHYSICAL COMPLAINTS:

Heart disorders, states of agitation, weakness of the nerves, sleeplessness, anxiety attacks, circulatory complaints, unconsciousness

EMOTIONAL COMPLAINTS:

Lack of self-confidence, insecurity, mourning, feelings of hatred, anger, disappointment, false expectations

Small-Intestine Meridian

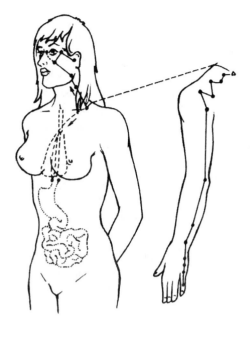

The small-intestine channel begins at the outer edge of the nail bed of the little finger, flows along the edge of the hand into the wrist, and continues along the back side of the lower arm to the elbow, the upper arm, and over the shoulder to the highest point on the back. One branch runs on the inside through the heart, diaphragm, and stomach to the small intestine. The other branch rises at the side of the neck to the cheek and flows up into the ear. A short branch forks off from the cheek and flows to the inner corners of the eye, where it unites with the subsequent bladder meridian.

▸▸ **Flowing Light:** Enjoyment of life, a feeling of being accepted, sense of security

▸▸| **Blocked Light:**

PHYSICAL COMPLAINTS:
> Digestive complaints, inflammations in the jaw area, pain in the arm, upper back region or in the shoulders, tinnitus, tension in the neck, feeling of numbness in the fingers

EMOTIONAL COMPLAINTS:
> Worries, hypersensitivity, sadness, concerns

Bladder Meridian

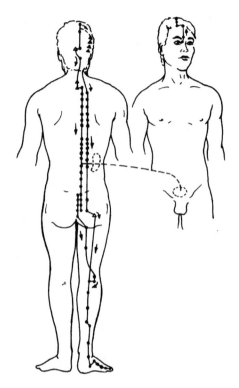

From the inner corners of the eye, the bladder meridian rises up over the forehead to the vertex of the head. A small branch enters the brain. The main branch flows over the back of the head to the neck. From there, the two or four branches respectively flow downward parallel to the spinal column. In the groin area, a branch forks off into the inside of the body to the kidneys and bladder. Both branches flow over the buttocks on the back side of the thighs downward into the hollow of the knee. This is where the two unite, and the main current flows into the calf to the outer ankle, along the outer side of the foot to the tip of the little toe. This is where it connects with the kidney channel.

▸▸ **Flowing Light:** Peace, trust, courage

▸▸▎ **Blocked Light:**

PHYSICAL COMPLAINTS:
> Headache, eye weakness, neck tension, backache, sciatica, urogenital health disorders

EMOTIONAL COMPLAINTS:
> Fears, nervousness, impatience, frustration, terror

Kidney Meridian

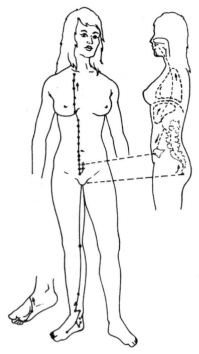

The kidney channel originates on the lower side of the little toe and flows into the center of the sole of the foot and along the instep to the inner ankle. From there, the energy flow rises on the inner side of the lower leg up to the knee, along the back inner side of the thighs upward, and enters the body close to the base of the spinal column to flow toward the kidneys and the bladder. Then the kidney meridian flows along the pubic bone over the belly and the chest upward toward the collarbone. A small branch begins in the kidney, rises up through the liver, diaphragm, and lungs, runs along the throat to the root of the tongue. An additional branch connects the lungs with the heart and merges with the heart-constrictor meridian.

▸▸ **Flowing Light:** Trust, firmness, creativity, carefreeness, self-confidence

▸▸▎ **Blocked Light:**

PHYSICAL COMPLAINTS:
> Urogenital disorders, muscle weakness of the legs, water congestion, disturbance of the sense of balance, kidney and bladder inflammations, bedwetting, impotence, backache, menstruation disorders, ear disorders

EMOTIONAL COMPLAINTS:
> Fearfulness, superstition, excessive caution, inner tension

Heart-Constrictor (Pericardium) Meridian

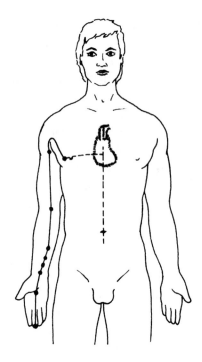

The heart-constrictor or pericardium meridian begins in the heart, descends through the diaphragm and connects the upper, middle, and lower section of the triple heater. A second branch flows into the rib area. It flows around the armpit along the inner side of the upper arm to the crook of the arm and over the lower arm to the palm of the hand and out to the tip of the middle finger. In the palm of the hand, a short branch forks off and connects at the nail bed of the ring finger with the triple heater.

➠ **Flowing Light:** Inner peace, relaxation, self-confidence, contentment

▶▶ **Blocked Light:**

PHYSICAL COMPLAINTS:

Brain disorders, migraine, epilepsy, nausea and vomiting, angina pectoris, hiccups, circulatory disorders, paralysis, states of exhaustion, circulatory collapse or state of shock

EMOTIONAL COMPLAINTS:

Melancholy, feelings of guilt, gloominess, jealousy, agitation, feelings of tension

Triple-Heater Meridian

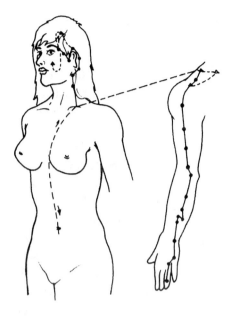

The triple-heater channel flows from the outer side of the ring finger over the back of the hand to the wrist, up the lower arm, over the elbow to the back side of the upper arm and the back side of the shoulder. From there, it rises over the shoulder and flows under the sternum into the chest. The inner branch leads through the heart constrictor (heart sac) into the diaphragm and unites the levels of the upper, middle, and lower heater (abdomen–stomach area–chest). An outer branch flows upward at the side of the neck, runs along the back edge of the ear, and inwardly circles the face. A small branch leads through the ear and rises to the surface in front of the ear. It moves upward to the outer end of the eyebrow and merges there with the gallbladder meridian.

➤➤ **Flowing Light:** Lightness, cheerfulness, equilibrium, confidence

➤➤ **Blocked Light:**

PHYSICAL COMPLAINTS:
> Health disorders of the ear, disturbance of the sense of balance, tinnitus, pain in the joints, pain in the arm or the shoulders, unbalanced body heat, digestive complaints, state of exhaustion

EMOTIONAL COMPLAINTS:
> Despair, hopelessness, loneliness, melancholy, burn-out syndrome

Gallbladder Meridian

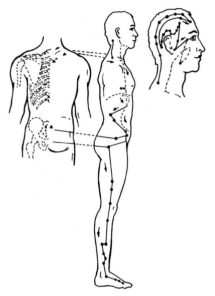

The gallbladder channel flows out of two branches away from the outer corners of the eye. One branch zigzags over the side of the head and flows behind the ear through the neck to the shoulder. From there it continues downward along the lower ribs to the hip area. The second branch flows into the body through the cheek, then runs downward over the neck and chest to the liver and gallbladder. In the hip area, it connects with the other branch. The energy channel then leads through the hip joint at the outer edge of the thighs to the knee, along the lower leg to the outer malleoli over the instep to the tip of the fourth toe. On the instep, a small branch forks diagonally across the foot to the big toe and brings the energy to the liver meridian.

▸▸ **Flowing Light:** Modesty, understanding, tolerance, lenience, initiative, creativity

▸▸▎ **Blocked Light:**

PHYSICAL COMPLAINTS:

Eye and ear disorders, headache, neck tension, lower-back pain, tightness in the chest, liver and gallbladder disorders, pain in the hip joint and knee, congestion in the legs

EMOTIONAL COMPLAINTS:

Anger, aggravation, indecisiveness, helplessness

Liver Meridian

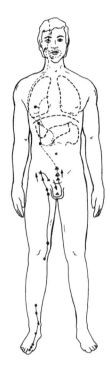

The liver meridian begins at the nail bed on the inner side of the big toe. It flows over the foot in front of the inner ankle to the inner side of the lower legs, then up through the knee to the thigh and the pubic region. It circles the genitals and enters the abdomen. Inside the body, the energy flows to the liver and gallbladder. It becomes frayed under the ribs before it pours into the lungs, where the cycle closes with the lung channel. The cycle of the energy-circulation system begins anew from here. A newly formed branch runs along the windpipe to the throat and on to the eye. From here, it flows downward over the cheek and circles the inside of the lips. The other branch rises up over the forehead to the vertex of the skull.

▸▸ **Flowing Light:** Contentment, ability to forgive, feeling of happiness, courage in life

▸▸▎ **Blocked Light:**

PHYSICAL COMPLAINTS:

Migraine, pain in the chest area and back, menstruation disorders, liver and gallbladder problems, digestive complaints, inflammation of the urinary tract, dysuria (problems with urination), impotence, pain in the lower leg, high blood pressure, epilepsy.

EMOTIONAL COMPLAINTS:

Anger, rage, resentment, aggravation, desire for revenge

Governor Vessel (Du-Mai*)

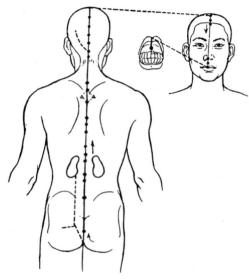

The governor vessel originates in the pelvic cavity and rises through an inner branch to the kidneys. Through another inner branch, the Light current flows downward to the perineum and rises to the surface there. It flows to the coccyx, up along the center of the spinal column to the head and brain. Over the crown of the head, the main current leads to the forehead and nose and ends in the upper gums.

⏩ **Flowing Light:** Enjoyment of life, initiative, inner balance, calmness

⏩ **Blocked Light:**

PHYSICAL COMPLAINTS:
> Infectious diseases, colds, nosebleeding, headache, backache, fatigue, bronchitis, weak nerves, urogenital disorders

EMOTIONAL COMPLAINTS:
> Depression, discouragement, lack of drive

---

*Pictures on page 146 and 147 are from Ted J. Kaptchuk, *Das große Buch der chinesischen Medizin*, O.W. Barth 1983.

Conception or Server Vessel (Ren-Mai)

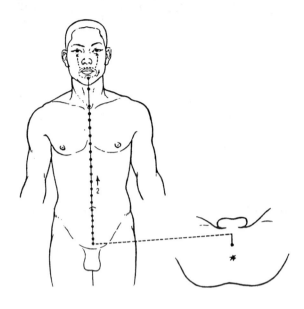

Coming from the pelvic cavity, it rises to the body surface at the perineum in the anal region. From there, it flows over the genitals to the front, rises across the center of the abdomen to the chest and over the throat to the lower jaw. Here the Light current penetrates inward, circles the lips and sends two branches to the eyes.

▶▶ **Flowing Light:** Calmness, inner peace, self-confidence, sense of responsibility, trust, openness

▶▶│ **Blocked Light:**

PHYSICAL COMPLAINTS:
>   Digestive disorders, heart and lung disorders, speech disorders, paralysis of the face, bronchitis, hoarseness, asthma, high blood pressure, impotence, flatulence, frigidity, abdominal pain, urogenital complaints

EMOTIONAL COMPLAINTS:
>   Feelings of shame, blushing, tension, tightness in the chest

---

Summary:
The 14 Steps of Light-Channel Healing

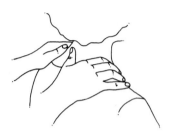

1. The shoulder-neck area

2. The entire spinal column

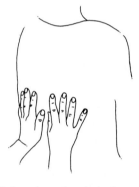

3. Smooth out the spinal column

4. Balance the aura and chakras

5. Neck, throat, and back of the head

6. Entire forehead area

7. Head points

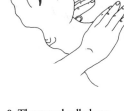

8. Throat and collarbone

9. Upper arms and shoulder joints

10. Closing the aura above the head

11. Arms and finger points

12. Knees and lower legs

13. Ankles and feet

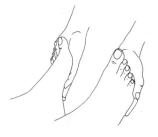

14. Giving thanks and concluding

Summary: Light-Channel Work for Self-Healing

The fingertips

"Praying hands"

Touching the face

Releasing the back of the head

Light-Channel work on the collarbone

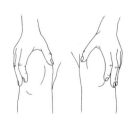

Light-Channel work on the knees

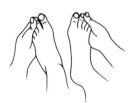

The tips of the toes

Touching the sternum

150

Summary: Light Channels

6 meridians with yang energy and 1 main vessel for all yang meridians

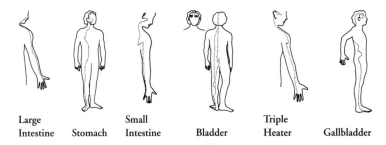

| Large Intestine | Stomach | Small Intestine | Bladder | Triple Heater | Gallbladder |

Governor or Directing Vessel

6 meridians with yin energy and 1 main vessel for all yin meridians

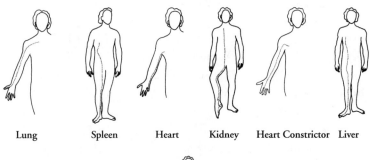

| Lung | Spleen | Heart | Kidney | Heart Constrictor | Liver |

Conception or Server Vessel

151

Physical Disorders and Corresponding Meridians

Abdominal pain . . . . . . LV-LI-SI-ST-GB
Agitation . . . . HC
Allergies . . . . SP-ST
Angina pectoris. . . . . . . HC
Ankle pain . . . . GB-BL-ST
Asthma. . . . . LU-ST-SP

Backache . . . . GB-BL-GV-SI
Bell's palsy . . . . LU-ST-LI-SI
Bladder inflammation. . BL-KI
Blood pressure, high . . . KI-LV-GB-ST-CV
Blood pressure, low. . . . CV
Bronchitis. . . . . LU-ST-CV-LI

Circulatory collapse . . . HC-HE-GV
Circulatory disorders . . HC-HE-TH
Colds . . . . LI-ST-LU
Coughing . . . . LU-ST

Deafness, partial . . . . . . TH-SI-KI
Diarrhea . . . . LI-LU-ST
Digestive complaints. . . SP-LV-ST-GB
Dizziness . . . . BL-ST-TH-GB

Eczema. . . . . ST-SP
Elbow pain . . . . LU-SI-TH
Epilepsy . . . . KI-LV-GV
Eye disorders. . . . . BL-LV-GB
Exhaustion . . . . HC-TH-ST

Facial muscle tension . . LI-ST-GB
Fatigue CV

Explanation of Abbreviations

BL Bladder Meridian
CV Conception Vessel
GB Gallbladder Meridian
GV Governor Vessel
HC Heart-Constrictor Meridian
HE Heart Meridian
KI Kidney Meridian
LU Lung Meridian
LI Large-Intestine Meridian
LV Liver Meridian
SI Small-Intestine Meridian
SP Spleen Meridian
ST Stomach Meridian
TH Triple Heater

Feeling of numbness... SI-TH-HE
Fever................ TH-LI-GV
Flatulence........... SP-GB-ST-LV
Foot complaints ...... SP-GB-ST-BL
Frigidity .... LV-HC
Frontal sinusitis ...... ST-TH-GB

Gallbladder weakness .. LV-GB
Gouty toe........... SP-LV

Headache .... ST-GB-BL-KI-LV
Heart pain .... HE-SP-SI
Heart palpitations..... HE-HC-SP
Heel pain .... BL-KI
Hemorrhoids .... SP-ST-LI
Hepatitis............ LV-GB
Hiccups .... HC
Hip-joint pain .... GB
Hoarseness .... CV-ST-LU

Impotence .... SP-LV-KI-CV
Incontinence......... BL-CV
Inflammation of
the bowels........... SP-LV-SI-ST

Joint pain .... TH-LI

Kidney inflammation .. KI-BL
Knee complaints...... SP-ST-GB

Legs, tired........... ST-GB-BL
Liver weakness .... LV-GB
Lower-back pain...... GB-BL
Lumbago .... GV-GB-BL-KI

Menopausal complaints SP-CV-LV

Menstrual complaints	SP-ST-KI-LV-CV
Migraine	ST-GB-BL-CV
Muscle spasms	BL-ST-SP
Nausea	HC
Neck blockage	SI-GB-BL-TH
Nervousness	GV-CV-HC
Neuralgia	GB
Nightmares	HE
Nosebleeding	GV
Nose, congested	LI-ST
Overweight	ST-SP
Rash	LI-ST-SP
Sciatica	BL-GB-KI-ST
Shortness of breath	LU-HC-ST
Shoulder pain	SI-TH-LI
Skin disorders	ST-SP
Sleeplessness	SP-BL-GB-LV-HE
Sore throat	ST-KI-LU-LV
Stomach complaints	ST-CV-SP-LI
Throat blockage	LU-ST
Tinnitus	GB-TH-SI-CV
Toothache	LI-ST-SI
Trigeminal neuralgia	TH-LI-ST-SI
Unconsciousness	HE-HC
Upper-abdomen pain	SP-ST-LV-GB
Urogenital disorders	GV-CV-LV-KI-BL
Vein complaints	SP-LV-ST-GB
Vision disorders	BL-LV-GB

Acknowledgements

My spiritual helpers have brought me together with loving, supportive people. So I would first like to thank you, my heavenly helpers, for your guidance through this life. You have often paved the way for me and given me signs.

One of these loving earthly helpers is *Karin Vial,* my agent and editor. After completing my training seminars, she encouraged me to make Light-Channel Healing accessible to many people by writing this book. She also wrote and directed our video on Light-Channel Healing. I extend my heartfelt thanks for her warm and enduring support, as well as for her deep understanding of the spiritual truths.

I would also like to give my special thanks to my daughter *Alexandra Fink-Thali* for enhancing and elaborating my sketches. She comprehended the text completely and enriched it with her beautiful illustrations.

I would like to thank *Bruno Thali,* my husband, for giving me the freedom and independence to fulfill my purpose in life.

I would like to express my sincere gratitude to all of the seminar participants who have trained with me in recent years. Their positive feedback definitively convinced me of the healing effects of this new method of treatment. It is with gratitude that I remember the beautiful experiences and openings to the Light in which I was allowed to participate during the training seminars.

Recommended Reading

In English language:

Clifford, Terry, *Tibetan Buddhist Medicine and Psychiatry*, Samuel Weiser 1984.

Eckert, Achim, *Chinese Medicine for Beginners: Use the Power of the Five Elements to Heal Body and Soul*, Prima Lifestyles, 1996.

Endo, Ryokyu, *Tao Shiatsu, Life Medicine for the Twenty-First Century*, Japan Publications, 1995.

Kaptchuk, Ted J., *Chinese Medicine*, Rider, New Edition 1985.

Melchizedek, Drunvalo, *The Ancient Secret of the Flower of Life*, Volume 1 and 2, Light Technology Publishing 1999.

Roob, Alexander, *Alchemy & Mysticism*, Taschen 2001.

Sagan, Samuel, *Planetary Forces*, Clairvision 1996.

Thali, Trudi, Instructional DVD on *Light-Channel Healing*, ISBN 3-9522439-8-1, Vitznau 2005.

Tashira, Tachi-ren, *What Is Lightbody?* New Leaf 1999.

In German language:

Fiedeler, Frank, *Yin und Yang*, Diederichs 2003.

Frank, Kai-Uwe, *Altchinesische Heilungswege*, Oesch 2003.

Heidemann, Christel, *Meridian-Therapie*, Volumes 1–3, Badenwhiler 1995.

Hempen, Carl-Hermann, *dtv-Atlas Akupunktur*, dtv 2000.

Hinrichs, Ulrike, *Die grossen Erzengelkarten*, Windpferd 2000.

Penzel, W., *Akupunkt-Massage nach Penzel*, Volumes 1–3, Eigenverlag W. Penzel 1993.

Perk, Johann, *Das Neue Testament*, Benziger Verlag, Einsiedeln.

Pollock, Maud N., *Vom Herzen durch die Hände*, Verlag Hermann Bauer 1995.

Rappenecker, Wilfried, *Fuenf Elemente und Zwoelf Meridiane*, Felicitas Hübner Verlag 1995.

Thali, Trudi,
- *Meridian-Karten für Lichtbahnen-Therapie*, Windpferd Verlag 2003.
- *Lichtfunken, Engelbotschaften*, Windpferd Verlag 2003.
- *Die 8 Wege Jesu zum Glück*, Kösel Verlag 2003.
- *Lichtbahnen Selbstheilung*, Windpferd Verlag, 2005.
- *Das Vaterunser als Chakra-Meditation*, ISBN 3-9522439-4-9.
- *Die Offenbarung des Johannes*, ISBN 3-9522439-5-7.
- *Entfaltung des Lichtbewusstseins*, (guided meditation on CD), Windpferd Verlag, 2005.

Ulrich, Dr. med. Wolf, *Schmerzfrei durch Akupressur*, Econ Verlag 1975.

Wang, Dr. Qin, *Gesund durch chinesische Medizin*, Karl F. Haug Verlag 1994.

About the Author

Trudi Thali, intuitive healer, author, and seminar leader, has worked for many years as a holistic health practitioner at her own office in Vitznau on Lake Lucerne in Switzerland. Intense transformational experiences led her to the spiritual path. Her special gift is the clairsentient perception of human and natural energetic states.

Trudi Thali has completed various trainings in the fields of *spiritual healing, meditation, sensitivity,* and *psychic abilities.* She leads meditation groups and seminars on a variety of spiritual topics on a regular basis. For many years, she has also trained professional health practitioners, therapists, and interested laypeople in the system of Light-Channel Healing that she has developed.

An instructional DVD on *Light-Channel Healing*, (with English soundtrack), ISBN 3-9522439-8-1, Vitznau 2005, has been released. Further information at www.trudi-thali.ch.

In addition, she has created a large number of pictures and mandalas with colored charcoal and pencils inspired by the divine geometry (exhibition in Lucerne in 1993).

Seminar programs and a list of Light-Channel Healing practitioners can be obtained from the author:

Trudi Thali
email: info@trudi-thali.ch
www.trudi-thali.ch

Frank Arjava Petter · Tadao Yamaguchi
Chujiro Hayashi

The Hayashi Reiki Manual

Traditional Japanese Healing Techniques from the Founder of the Western Reiki System

Dr. Chujiro Hayashi is the highly renowned student of Reiki founder, Dr. Mikao Usui. Dr. Hayashi developed his own style of Reiki and became the teacher of Hawayo Takata, who introduced Reiki to the West.
However, Dr. Hayashi also taught Reiki to Japanese students such as young Chiyoko Yamaguchi, born in 1920. She is still practicing today—and Frank Arjava Petter was allowed to become her student and learn the original Hayashi Reiki system from her.
The manual presents the story of Dr. Hayashi, newly researched and sensationally illustrated with previously unpublished archive photos, Reiki techniques never taught in the West before, and specific documents such as the original certificates of Dr. Hayashi.

full color ·112 pages · $19.95
ISBN 0-914955-75-6

Walter Lübeck · Frank Arjava Petter

Reiki
Best Practices

Wonderful Tools of Healing for the First, Second and Third Degree of Reiki

Western Reiki techniques—published and presented in great detail for the first time

The internationally renowned Reiki Masters Walter Lübeck and Frank Arjava Petter introduce primarily Western Reiki techniques and place a valuable tool in the hands of every Reiki practitioner for applying Reiki in a specific and effective way for protection and healing.
A total of 60 techniques, such as: aura massage with Reiki, deprogramming of old patterns, karma clearing, protecting against energy loss, Tantra with Reiki are exclusively presented and described in detail for the first time in this fascinating guide.

296 pages · $19.95
ISBN 0-914955-74-8

Rendered by Li Jun Feng

Sheng Zhen Wuji Yuan Gong

A Return to Oneness · Qigong of Unconditional Love

To embark on the practice of *Wuji Yuan Gong* is to begin a journey of rediscovery—a journey back to one's true home.

Home is not just a place, or structure, or people. It is a state of consciousness where one experiences a sense of oneness. To return to one's true home is to return to one's original nature—to rediscover one's real Self.

The journey back to one's true home is a journey into one's own Heart—a journey into the heart of existence— back to that "nothingness" from which everything arises. To attain this state is to know one's place in the scheme of things—to always be at home no matter where one is—to always experience wholeness no matter what circumstances on one's life may be. To attain this state is to merge with all and to know that there is only ONE.

fully illustrated with black&white photographs ·202 pages · $24.95
ISBN 0-914955-77-2

Merlin's Magic

Yoga and Ayurveda · Music for a Healing Space

Yoga and Ayurveda developed together and are therefore inseparable. They have the power to permeate your life on the physical and the spiritual level. *Ayurveda* relieves physical and emotional complaints and brings you into harmony with your body. *Yoga* opens the spiritual plane, all the way up to the highest level of self-realization. Merlin's Magic is one of the most renowned composers of spiritual healing music throughout the world. The heart of Merlin's Magic is producer and composer Andreas Mock, whose unique style of gently flowing melodies and meditative magic is splendidly supported by various outstanding musicians. Andreas always enjoys creating music in cooperation with distinguished experts from a variety of healing modalities.

64 minute CD · $16.95
ISBN: 0-910261-21-0

Herbs and other natural health products and information are often available at natural food stores or metaphysical bookstores. If you cannot find what you need locally, you can contact one of the following sources of supply.

Sources of Supply:

The following companies have an extensive selection of useful products and a long track-record of fulfillment.They have natural body care, aromatherapy, flower essences, crystals and tumbled stones, homeopathy, herbal products, vitamins and supplements, videos, books, audio tapes, candles, incense and bulk herbs, teas, massage tools and products and numerous alternative health items across a wide range of categories.

WHOLESALE:

Wholesale suppliers sell to stores and practitioners, not to individual consumers buying for their own personal use. Individual consumers should contact the RETAIL supplier listed below. Wholesale accounts should contact with business name, resale number or practitioner license in order to obtain a wholesale catalog and set up an account.

Lotus Light Enterprises, Inc.

PO Box 1008 LCH
Silver Lake, WI 53170 USA
262 889 8501 (phone)
262 889 8591 (fax)
800 548 3824 (toll free order line)

RETAIL:

Retail suppliers provide products by mail order direct to consumers for their personal use. Stores or practitioners should contact the wholesale supplier listed above.

Internatural

PO Box 489 LCH
Twin Lakes, WI 53181 USA
800 643 4221 (toll free order line)
262 889 8581 office phone
EMAIL: internatural@internatural.com
WEB SITE: www.internatural.com

Web site includes an extensive annotated catalog of more than 14,000 items that can be ordered "on line" for your convenience 24 hours a day, 7 days a week.